An Unlikely Scholar

Nancy VanDermark

BookLocker

Paperback ISBN: 978-1-64438-176-2
Hardcover ISBN: 978-1-64438-177-9

Published by BookLocker.com, Inc., St. Petersburg, Florida.

Printed on acid-free paper.

A few of the names have been changed to respect the privacy of the individuals.

BookLocker.com, Inc.
2018

First Edition

Dedication

To Peter and Helena,
All My Love,
Always and All Ways

I imagine the earth when I am no more:

nothing happens, no loss, it's still a strange pageant,

women's dresses, dewy lilacs, a song in the valley.

Yet the books will be there on the shelves, well born,

derived from people, but also from radiance, heights.

(Last lines of a poem by Czeslaw Milosz).

No Other Way

Could we but see the pattern of our days,
we should discern how devious were the
ways
by which we came to this, the present time,
this place in life; and we should see the
climb
our soul has made up through the years.
We should forget the hurts, the wanderings,
the fears,
the wastelands of our life, and know
that we could come no other way or grow
into our good without these steps our feet
found hard to take, our faith found hard to
meet.
The road of life winds on, and we like
travelers go
from turn to turn until we come to know
the truth that life is endless and that we
forever are inhabitants of all eternity.

-Martha Smock

Chapter One

"Without leaps of imagination or dreaming,
we lose the excitement of possibilities.
Dreaming, after all, is a form of planning."
-Gloria Steinem

January 1988

I boarded the 7:20 a.m. Trailways bus in Wilkes-Barre bound for Port Authority. It was a typical January morning in northeastern Pennsylvania, cold and damp with a monochromatic gray sky that merged into the pavement on Interstate 80. This was a well-planned semi-annual shopping trip, and I settled back into my seat to consider a strategy that would maximize time and money. I wore a navy blue Christian Dior military style coat and a one-carat pear-shaped cubic zirconia ring. Tucked inside my faux Fendi purse was a $100 bill and a Diner's Club credit card.

Arriving at Saks Fifth Avenue shortly after 10:00 a.m., I walked back to the Estée Lauder counter on a mission to bring home a new fragrance and something from the Spring makeup collection. As I approached the counter, I saw a well-dressed woman in a full-length mink coat speaking with a sales associate. "Is there something else I can show you today, Mrs. Lauder?" the associate inquired politely. I could hardly believe my eyes – it was Estée Lauder herself!

The queen of cosmetics was tall, with perfectly coiffed dark blonde hair. At nearly eighty years old she was still a striking woman. As she turned to walk away, I impulsively spoke up. "Mrs. Lauder, I just want to tell you that I think Paulina Poriskova is the most phenomenal spokeswoman you have ever hired!"

Paulina Porizkova is a Czech super-model who became the face of Estée Lauder in 1988, winning an unheard of $6,000,000 contract. Her ads were sensual, a dramatic departure from the company's traditionally demure town and country style images.

Mrs. Lauder's reply altered the trajectory of my life. "Well, thank you. You're quite lovely yourself."

The bus ride home gave me time to reflect on dreams that had died; some killed, others buried alive. I was unprepared for the power of a dream that sought to be resurrected by its own force.

Estée Lauder said that I was lovely; I hadn't felt lovely. In fact, I had begun acquiring symbols of perceived affluence – the designer coat, fake accessories and more than the usual amount of makeup to cover my insecurities. I was the only person in my husband's immediate and extended family without a college education. This wasn't the first time that I had used glamour as an effective and deliberate disguise, and it wouldn't be the last.

September 1972

I began my senior year of high school at sixteen while working part-time for the same party favor factory in Pittston, Pennsylvania that had employed me for the past two years. Throughout the summer, I worked full-time on the assembly line, from 7 a.m. to 3 p.m. My job was gluing tops on party horns. I had to test one every hundred or so. The job had allowed me to save enough money to attend the Marilyn Gauntlett Modeling and Finishing School in Wilkes-Barre. The nine month certificate course curriculum included walking, speaking, modeling and etiquette, and promised employment to qualified graduates. For years, I had studied *Glamour* and *Cosmopolitan* magazines religiously, carefully crafting a personality cultivated by Helen Gurley Brown and Gloria Steinem.

Helen Gurley Brown, the iconic editor of *Cosmo*, had turned the publication into a self-help guide for working girls. She gave advice on everything from makeup and money to how to please a man. Gloria

Steinem, after graduating from Smith College in 1956, became a journalist writing essays for *Glamour* and *New York* magazine. She eventually became a co-founder of *Ms.* magazine. I imagined these women as powerful older sisters and regularly consulted their articles and essays for advice.

In the 1960's, best-selling fashion magazines featured a section on vocational training schools and junior colleges. There were ads for airline and secretarial schools as well as short courses in modeling and fashion related careers. An ad on a matchbook cover read, "Be a Model or Just Look Like One." I dreamed that one day I would find an exciting job and leave the northeastern Pennsylvania coal region.

At sixteen, my fashion sense left much to be desired, but the instructors at the Gauntlett School provided excellent guidance and I was an eager student. As a college prep "C" student with straight A's in geometry, Spanish and typing, my after-school hours were spent on factory work and modeling school. After scoring 980 on the SAT, the guidance counselor at Wyoming Area High School called me into her office and questioned why I had not yet applied to any colleges.

"Dr. Wiley," I replied determinedly, "I just don't want to be poor anymore. I'm going to work full-time as a secretary."

I was an 80 word-per-minute typist with a reasonably respectable I.Q. and I already had plans. A clerical job would function as my stepping stone to a well-paid position as an executive secretary.

There had been no discussion of student loans with the guidance counselor, nor were there any conversations at home about my attending college.

Chapter Two

"We are braver and wiser because they existed, those strong women and men...We are who we are because they were who they were. It's wise to know where you come from, who called your name."

-Dr. Maya Angelou

The VanDermark family can trace its roots to Germany, where the original name was von der Marck.

Comte' de La Marck (the County of Marck) was a county and state of the Holy Roman Empire. Altena Castle was built in the early 12th century, as a stronghold by members of German nobility, the older Counts of Berg. After the distribution of the Berg family estates in 1161, Altena became the center of the County of Altena. Eberhard I, was Count of Berg-Altena. In 1180, after the death of Eberhard, the estate was divided between his two sons, Arnold and Friedrich. Friedrich then came into possession of Oberhof Marck, a mayor manor (large estate without fortifications) in the village of Marck. A dozen or so years later, in about 1198, Friedrich built the Castle of Marck. In 1202, Friedrich's son, Adolf, still a young man, began to identify himself simply as Adolf "von der Marck" (literal translation "from the Marck"). Adolf eventually simplified and shortened his formal and quite lengthy title from Adolf I, Count of Altena-Mark and Krickenbeck, and instead opted to use Count of the Marck. The Counts of the Marck were among the most powerful and influential Westphalian lords in the Holy Roman Empire. Following the year 1226, Adolf was successful in reuniting the extensive former family lands of the Counts of Berg-Altena. At the height of their power, the family also ruled the four duchies of Julich, Cleves, Berg and Guelders as well as the county of Ravensberg.[1]

Anne of Cleves, briefly the wife of England's Henry VIII, is one of the most renowned figures in history and was a direct descendant of the main line of the House of La Marck.

Anne of Cleves is my distant cousin on the VanDermark side. She became Henry VIII's fourth wife and was the Queen of England from January 6th to July 9th 1540.

According to *History Extra*:

Anne arrived at Rochester Castle, in Kent, on a stormy New Year's Eve. Henry was horrified when he saw her, shouting to Thomas Cromwell, his chief minister, *"I like her not! I like her not!"* Apparently, Anne's portrait disguised the reality of her physical appearance. Unlike Henry's first three wives, Anne was big boned with a large nose and skin that had been pitted from smallpox.

On their wedding night, according to a detailed account, the king went so far as to run his hands all over Anne's body, but found himself incapable of doing anything more. The next morning, he told Cromwell (whom he later had decapitated) that she had a *"very evil smell about her"* and he was unable *"to know her carnally."* Consequently, King Henry VIII left Anne of Cleves *"as good a maid as I found her."*

Anne complied with the annulment of her marriage to the king and was richly rewarded. She was given a palace, a manor and an annual income. Additionally, she was allowed to keep all of her royal jewels, as well as plate and goods to furnish her new properties. Anne was exalted to a status as the king's sister which took precedence over all of his subjects except for his children and future wives.

He subsequently gave her Hever Castle, the former home of Anne Boleyn, which became her principal residence. *"It says much for Anne's strength of character that she managed to accept and adapt to her new life with dignity."*[2]

The original Marck spelling eventually gave way to the colloquialism, "Mark" and, at some point in time, the name Von Der Mark was further misspelled as VanDermark, quite likely in the mid-1600's during an ancestor's emigration from Europe to New York.

Thomas VanDermark, the progenitor of the VanDermark Family in America, arrived in New York on one of Henry Hudson's ships and settled in Kingston, Ulster County, New York, around 1665. He moved to the new settlement of Marbletown where he died in 1724 at age 81. He married Jacomyntje Jacobs about 1674. She died April 2, 1693. The VanDermarks had ten children.

My grandfather, Emmit William VanDermark Sr., was born in 1890. In 1913, he married Emma Decker in her hometown of Lopez, Pennsylvania. The couple moved to Johnson City, New York where both became employees of the Endicott Johnson Shoe Company. The VanDermarks had five children; four of whom survived beyond infancy. My father, Emmit Jr. born in July of 1917, was the eldest son. As the family grew, Emma's parents moved in with their daughter's family to help care for the children.

After 17 years of marriage, Emma Decker VanDermark contracted pneumonia and died suddenly in 1930. At the time of his mother's death, my father, an excellent student, was in the eighth grade. Concurrent with the tragic loss of Emma's life was the crippling financial blow to what had been an eight member household. Emma's important contribution to the family income was now gone.

Unable to cope with the loss of his beloved wife, the unaccustomed role of single parent, (Emma's mother had also died) and the financial strain, my grandfather, Emmit Sr., began drinking heavily. He made a series of decisions which radically affected the trajectory of his family's future. He abruptly left his job and moved himself and his four children to the coal region of northeastern Pennsylvania. My father was forced to drop out of school at the age of thirteen to help support their newly motherless family. His maternal grandfather, 69-year-old John Decker, left behind in the move, found it necessary to move to a convalescent home.

The stock market crash in October 1929, precipitated the Great Depression. "An unequal distribution of the nation's wealth – in 1929,

40 percent of the population received only 12.5 percent of the aggregate family income, while the top 5 percent of the population received 30 percent – meant that once the Depression began, the majority of people were unable to spend the amount of money that was needed to revive the economy. The Great Depression became self-perpetuating, and for ten years it left what one observer has called *'an invisible scar' running through the lives of millions of Americans."* By 1933, unemployment had reached 25 percent and the U.S. gross national product (GNP) was cut almost in half.[3]

Emmit Jr. joined his father and began working in the coal mines in Wyoming, Pennsylvania, while the younger children attended school. For seven years, my father had to use dynamite to blast coal from tight areas deep beneath the surface of the earth. When my grandfather exited the mile-deep cavern each workday he often drank all night, in beer gardens or at home. It was not unusual for him to drink away all of the family's rent money. When he couldn't pay the rent, he took the children to a new location in the middle of the night. During the years that Dad and his father worked in the mines, my grandfather moved his family forty-two times. Dad worked ten hours a day, six days a week, for fourteen cents an hour. After nearly a decade, my father was not just broke, he was broken.

In September of 1939, Nazi Germany attacked Poland. Although the United States had not yet entered the war, there was talk that a peacetime draft would soon be implemented. My father, Emmit VanDermark Jr., enlisted instead. He was 24 years old when he joined the Army in April of 1941, eight months before the U.S. formally entered World War II. Dad's intelligence and mechanical ability were quickly recognized by his superiors and he was promoted from Private First Class to Army Staff Sergeant.

In my father's eyes, the uniform had leveled the playing field. His work was important and his contributions were recognized. As a result, his confidence improved and his countenance reflected it.

Dad served with Company “A”, 816th Engineer Aviation Battalion U..S Army Corps of Engineers, in the European Theater. In 1942, his company was among the first American troops to arrive in England. The 816th Engineer Aviation Battalion built airstrips all across Europe, starting with A-3 in Normandy, right after D-Day.

“Of all the factors that helped the Allies win the war, none was more important than the unbroken flow of supplies to the front lines.” - *WarfareHistoryNetwork*

At one point, the 816th was building an airfield during some of the fiercest fighting on European soil, when much-needed mechanical supplies for the trucks were blocked from reaching “A” Company. Dad was in charge of the motor pool. Relying on intelligence reports and leading a handful of brave men, he staged a night-time raid on a Nazi-held warehouse which contained desperately needed automotive supplies. He and his small band of men successfully liberated those supplies for the benefit of the allies. Dad served until his Honorable Discharge in 1945. He was awarded the Bronze Star Medal for bravery in the face of danger.

After the war, my father took a correspondence course in diesel mechanics and later worked for a construction company in Forty Fort, Pennsylvania. Every evening, he would go downstairs to his basement workshop for hours, sleeping only four hours a night, before returning to work the next morning. After several years, he brought his “invention” upstairs to show my mother, sister and me what he had been working on. It was the first anti-lock, hydraulic brake system. My father had also collected years of newspaper articles that featured motor vehicle accidents involving brake failures. He hired Anthony J. Lupas Jr., a well-known Wilkes-Barre, Pennsylvania patent attorney who immediately recognized the potential value of the product.

Lupas prepared and filed the patent for my father. Then he went further. He had glossy brochures printed which explained all of the features and benefits of Dad's invention. He also independently assembled a group of potential investors who expressed interest in manufacturing the part for General Motors. The identity of the men who comprised that group of investors was not disclosed to my father at the time.

One day, the call my parents had been anxiously awaiting arrived. Attorney Lupas advised that General Motors was interested in Dad's invention and that an appointment had been set for Dad to make a presentation in Detroit. My father was told that he and Mr. Lupas would be traveling to the meeting in Detroit on a private plane, and that the investors would accompany them.

On the day that my father flew to Detroit, my mother planned the party that would launch Dad's successful venture, and of course, celebrate our transformation from poor to rich. We waited by the phone all evening for Dad's good news, but the call came rather late. My father told us that he would discuss the details with us when he arrived back home, but that the executives at General Motors had been excited about his amazing invention and had their engineers review the details. He said that GM wanted to put it in every new car and truck they manufactured.

My father had not been introduced to the potential investors that Attorney Lupas had assembled until the day of the flight to Detroit. When he was introduced, Dad immediately recognized their names. He had seen those names mentioned in the newspaper. They had well-known connections to organized crime.

It wasn't until the return flight from Detroit to Wilkes-Barre, that Attorney Lupas explained the details of the investor's proposal to my father. A manufacturing facility would be created and the investors would supply all of the necessary capital. In exchange, they expected to receive sixty percent of the net profit, leaving my father with the remaining forty.

Already suspicious as a result of his attorney's newly revealed affiliation with the criminal element, Dad continued to lose trust in his attorney in the days, weeks and months that followed. He began to suspect that the executives at GM were also untrustworthy.

My father's suspicions were eventually proven correct on both counts, and his dream of using his mechanical genius to save many lives and radically alter a few, slowly died. It was suspected that General Motors tweaked his invention's components slightly and patented it as their own invention.

General Motors is said to be the largest U.S. corporation with the most lawsuits against it for patent infringement. It is not financially feasible for the average inventor to maintain the lawyers' fees involved in pursuing such a lawsuit.

Karma eventually found Dad's attorney. Years later, Federal prosecutors accused attorney Anthony J. Lupas Jr. of running a multimillion-dollar Ponzi scheme targeting his own clients. Lupas was arrested, stood trial, and was sentenced to prison.

Chapter Three

"All of my youth, growing up in my Italian family, was focused around the table. That's where I learned about love."

-Dr. Leo Buscaglia

My mother's mantra, "We may not have money, but we're rich in spirit," was most assuredly charged with a spirit of optimism, derived primarily from her Italian culture, an innate "la dolce vita," and her strong belief in Dr. Norman Vincent Peale's *The Power of Positive Thinking*. Like my father, her strength was derived from adversity.

Mom grew up in a non-English speaking household with seven siblings. Her father, Luigi DeVergilio, was born in Monte Sant'Angelo, Italy, in March of 1890, and he immigrated to the United States when he was fourteen. He met my grandmother, Irene Barbata, who was born in August of 1895. She arrived in the United States from Serracapriola, when she was twenty-one, after the death of her fiance' in World War I. Irene and Luigi were introduced by friends while living in the Bronx, and they married shortly thereafter. They moved to Pittston, Pennsylvania, where Luigi had been promised the American dream – gainful employment and a home in which to raise a family. It was a coal mining "company" house, the rent for which was subsidized by working long hours for little pay, in the damp belly of the earth.

"Between around 1880 and 1924, more than four million Italians immigrated to the United States, half of them between 1900 and 1910 alone - the majority fleeing grinding rural poverty in southern Italy and Sicily."[4]

My grandmother, whose name was changed at Ellis Island from Erina to Irene, was illiterate and considered a "peasant class" immigrant. Except for her Italian friends, who still used Erina as her given name, everyone else called her Irene. My grandfather, Luigi, on the other hand, was bilingual. He was able to read and write, both in English as well as in Italian.

Irene and Luigi became active members of a newly established Protestant church led by Reverend James Turco, whose personal mission it was to convert Italian immigrants from Catholics to Protestants. He delivered his Sunday sermon in Italian and distributed Italian hymnals so that congregants could sing in their native tongue. Members were encouraged to find hope in the gospel of Jesus Christ by attending services regularly and studying the Bible at Sunday evening classes. The Second Presbyterian Church became the foundation of the DeVergilio's life in America. Despite grueling work in the mines and economic hardship, my grandparents supported the church from which they derived strength and a sense of community.

Irene planted fruit trees and a perennial garden overflowing with poppies, peonies, hydrangeas and roses. Her vegetable garden included tomatoes, squash, escarole, lettuce, beans and cucumbers. She served fresh vegetables during the summer and canned enough from her harvest to last throughout the winter and spring.

Irene's kitchen table was busy and bountiful. She turned a five-pound bag of flour into culinary works of art. The aroma of crusty, fresh baked bread intermingled with the scent of roses as one approached the front door. Early in the morning, after preparing the stove with coal and kindling, she savored a hot cup of coffee. By mid-morning, her table was filled with such homemade delicacies as noodles for chicken soup, ravioli, or pizza fritta – fried bread dough sprinkled with sugar.

Luigi became ill in the winter of 1931 when Irene was pregnant with their eighth child. He was diagnosed with tuberculosis and sent to a sanitarium in White Haven, where Irene visited him every Sunday. When the new baby was two months old, Luigi died at the age of 42, leaving Irene alone with eight children: three boys, Frank, Anthony, and Joseph, and five girls, Theresa, Mary, Josephine, Jean, and my mother, Helen DeVergilio.

Mining company rules stated that if a miner died while living in a company house, his oldest son was required to report to work immediately or the family would be evicted. Irene's oldest son, Frank, quit school and began work in the mines when he was fifteen in order to save the family's home.

A few months after Luigi died, three women showed up at Irene's door and identified themselves as representatives of the state welfare department. One of the women was a translator, who explained that the state wished to place Irene's children in foster care where they could better assimilate into American society.

In 1932, a mother who became a widow had no rights, and guardians were often appointed by the city and state Orphan's Court.

My grandmother pounded her fist on the kitchen table and exclaimed, "I will take all of my children back to Italy where my family will help me raise them, if you try to take even one child from my care!"

According to historians Ellen Carol DuBois and Lynn Dumenil:

"Immigrant mothers had responsibility for preserving customary ways against the tremendous forces working to Americanize them and their families. They continued to cook traditional foods and observe religious obligations, while their husbands and children entered into the American economic mainstream to make the family's living. As practices that were ancient and reflexive became deliberate and problematic, it fell to women to defend and perpetuate the old ways, thus laying the basis for what would eventually become American ethnic identity. Such practices constituted implicit resistance to the forces of Americanization and cultural homogenization." [5]

Members of the Second Presbyterian Church offered assistance to Irene and her family. Her youngest son, Joseph, attended Girard College in Philadelphia, founded in 1933, as a school for fatherless boys. With the exception of Frank, who continued working in the mines, all of Irene's children graduated from high school.

All three of Irene's sons served honorably in the United States Army during World War II. Joseph, Irene's youngest son, had been stationed near Bari, Italy when the war ended. My great-grandmother Barbata prepared a feast for Joseph and his comrades at the ancestral home in Serracapriola. The men were celebrated as heroes and were treated to the finest wine and traditional Italian delicacies before returning to their base.

On the way back, Joseph hit a tree with his Army Jeep and was killed instantly; his friends sustained injuries but survived. My mother has recounted the absolute horror of seeing two Army representatives walk up the pathway to my grandmother's house after the family had celebrated the survival of all three sons.

Mother said that my grandmother was so angry with God that she did not attend church for a year.

Joseph's body was the first returned to Pittston, by train, after the war had ended. Hundreds of people gathered at the train station to honor his service.

Chapter Four

"Early in life problems can be the yeast that makes you rise into bread!"
-Helen Gurley Brown

After their marriage, Emmit VanDermark Jr. and Helen DeVergilio had first lived with Helen's mother, Irene. The couple and their daughter moved into their own home in 1956.

Harding, Pennsylvania is a village along the Susquehanna River, located about ten miles north of Wilkes-Barre. On June 30, 1778, seven settlers were killed by a party of British soldiers and Native Americans. The settlers had been warned of an impending attack by *"British rangers, Seneca Indians and a rag-tag bunch of Tories"* and *"on the evening of June 30th, ...a group of settlers finishing up their chores in the field were set upon by the raiding party."*

Harding brothers Benjamin, 25, and Stukley, 23, were killed first, *"mercilessly tomahawked."* The Harding brothers' bodies are buried in West Pittston's Jenkins-Harding Cemetery. Years later, brother Elisha Harding had a monument erected over their grave with the inscription *"Sweet be the sleep of those who prefer death to slavery."* Nissley, Erin. "Local History: Harding Massacre of 1778," *The Times Tribune*, 29 June 2014.[6]

In 1956, less than a thousand people lived in the 13 square mile village. Most of the residents were farmers, whose crops fed workers in the Wyoming Valley's waning anthracite coal industry. Small cottages were located along the Sullivan Trail, where docks lined the riverbank for fishing and recreation. In the summer, residents and visitors enjoyed swimming and boating in the Susquehanna's crystal clear water.

Emmit and Helen bought a fully furnished two bedroom cottage with views of both the river and Campbell's Ledge, a picturesque local landmark, for the sum of $5,000. The house had been winterized, and

Emmit was relieved that his family would enjoy the comfort of a central, coal-fired, heating system.

The move was an enormous adjustment for Helen, who had spent her entire life in Pittston, where city services and public transportation were readily available. The VanDermark's new home had a rural delivery address, on Route 92, as there were no house numbers, street names or sidewalks. There was a general store two doors down that carried essential dry goods, grocery items, candy, hand dipped ice cream, and motor vehicle supplies. It was also the only gasoline service station in the village. Helen's mother, Irene, was utterly distraught over the young family's move and refused to speak to her daughter. Helen felt alone and isolated for the first time in her life.

In her best-selling book, *The Feminine Mystique*, Betty Friedan argued that millions of American women were suffering from *"the problem that has no name"* brought on by restricting women from aspiring toward anything outside of domestic life. Friedan writes that, *"We can no longer ignore that voice within women that says: 'I want something more than my husband and my children and my home.'"*

Friedan was highly critical of mass media for their constant suggestions that women exercise their creativity with new cake mixes and cleaning products while doctors prescribed tranquilizers for women's neuroticism. *The Feminine Mystique*, which sold more than 3 million copies, also criticized women's magazines for not providing the intellectual stimulation, through articles on politics and social issues, that readers deserved.

By contrast, scholars have noted that the feminine mystique was a problem that primarily affected affluent, white women living in suburbia. In fact, *Ebony*, the major African American popular magazine of the period *"featured women who fought racial discrimination and achieved success in business, politics, and the arts, although it was careful to note the importance of these women's family roles and their attention 'to the needs of their husbands and children.'"*

Historians, Ellen Carol DuBois and Lynn Dumenil further argue that Friedan overstated her case among middle-class white women. They write:

"...in contrast to Friedan's claim that magazines ignored women's discontent, they gave extensive attention to wives' dissatisfaction with their married lives and their housework obligations. In advice columns like the Ladies' Home Journal's 'Can This Marriage Be Saved?' letter writers testified to the drudgery of household chores and the stresses entailed in unrelenting domesticity. Nevertheless, the advice dispensed uniformly encouraged women to find psychological tools to help them adjust to the gendered expectations of middle-class marriage, rather than challenge the expectations themselves."[7]

The move to Harding was Helen's first experience living outside of her mother's home and, although the transition from city life was difficult, she had a spirit of determination and optimism that lightened the challenge. Once they were settled, Helen made friends with her new neighbors. She particularly liked Peg and "Bud" Fisher, an older couple who lived two doors away. The Fishers were unable to have children and had chosen not to adopt. Peg was a southern woman, a distant relative of the famous Kresge family. She impressed Helen with her perfect diction, grace and elegant stature. Peg played bridge weekly with her friends, and kept a meticulously clean and organized home. The Fishers tended to their rose garden every day throughout the summer. Peg's husband, "Bud" whose given name was Clarence, worked at the power plant a mile north on the river.

The VanDermark's immediate next door neighbors were an unusual bunch. On the north side was the Shirtz family. Ken Shirtz, Sr. and his son, Kenny, drank a lot of beer and both were morbidly obese. Mrs. Shirtz, who was rail thin, chain-smoked Tarryton cigarettes.

On the south side of the VanDermark cottage was a duplex. Half of the duplex was occupied by the Hoskins family: Reverend Hoskins, a Pentecostal minister, his wife, Suzie, and their two sons. The other half of the duplex was occupied by Mrs. Hoskins' mother Alma, an alcoholic. Alma once asked my father what his maiden name was. Reverend Hoskins had converted part of the basement of the duplex into a Pentecostal church where he conducted services on Sunday mornings and Wednesday evenings. Through our living room window, we could hear the congregants as they spoke loudly in tongues, waving their hands in the air. The remainder of the Hoskin's basement had been partitioned to create a one-room apartment for their tenant, a World War II veteran named Joe. Both of Joe's legs had been amputated during the war, leaving him confined to a wheelchair. Joe was also an alcoholic.

It wasn't until a year later, after Emmit and Helen welcomed their second daughter, Lynne, into the world, that Helen's mother, Irene, finally began visiting.

Emmit arose at five o'clock in the morning every weekday. He made coffee and brought it to Helen in bed, then left for work as a diesel mechanic for Sordoni Construction Company, returning around four-thirty in the afternoon. Helen was a busy mother and homemaker who developed a wonderful talent for cooking, baking and decorating. Every weeknight, Emmit and the girls were served a traditional "meat and potatoes" meal followed by a homemade cake or pie. On Saturdays, Emmit made breakfast and then drove Helen to the grocery store in town. The couple enjoyed antique hunting for pieces that Emmit restored. They often drove out toward the Red Rock mountain area to attend auctions. After purchasing an antique organ, Helen quickly learned to play all of her favorite church hymns by ear.

On Sunday mornings, Helen made traditional Italian style tomato sauce with meatballs and sausage, allowing it to simmer to perfection for hours. Emmit drove his two daughters to Sunday school in town, then drove back to Harding to dress for the church service in his finest suit, fedora, and wing tip shoes. Helen was always dressed beautifully for church and she proudly took her place in the pew with her family. Most Sundays, Grandma Irene joined our family for dinner, in Harding, which meant that my father drove to town and back three times. Once or twice a year, Dad treated us to Sunday dinner at the Chinese restaurant at the

Wilkes-Barre/Scranton Airport. Irene was always invited to join us but vowed she would never eat Chinese food.

My grandmother Irene didn't speak a word of English but it was abundantly clear to everyone that her resentment over the family's move from her home in the city still simmered. My mother and grandmother often got into heated arguments in Italian during dinner. As a result, my father developed a serious dislike for all things Italian, especially my grandmother. Dad habitually retreated to the basement immediately after finishing his meal, and would refuse to come back upstairs until it was time to drive his mother-in-law home. We sat quietly in the backseat of his enormous green 1954 Buick Special, until Irene was dropped off.

We were active members of the Second Presbyterian church, and my sister, Lynne, and I received pins at the end of most Sunday school years for perfect attendance. Our father served as an usher, Mom was vice-president of the women's Golden Star club, and she also served as a deacon. The church was the center of our social lives.

During the summer, we attended vacation Bible school at the small Church of Christ, located five doors away from our home. St. Pius Roman Catholic Church was a half mile away and, in July, hosted a three day bazaar. The church ladies served homemade ethnic specialties, such as perogies and stuffed cabbage, and the men organized pony rides and bingo.

I entered first grade at Harding Elementary School in 1959, when I was four years old. There were no kindergarten classes, nor were there restrictions on the age at which a child could begin elementary school. My sister, Lynne, on the other hand, was subject to new laws governing age restrictions, which placed her three school years behind me. The small, red brick school we attended was set back on Mount Zion Road, five miles from home. Mrs. Dymond, a kind woman who loved children, was my first grade teacher; her husband, Don, ran the general store.

In 1960, when I was in second grade, my mother decided that we should move to a larger home. While we were in school and Dad was at work, she made arrangements with Mr. Hess, the owner of a stately, older home directly across the street from our cottage, for us to move in, pending the sale of our own home. The agreement also included the arrangement for Mr. Hess to live with our family indefinitely. He became actively involved with our family life, driving my mother to town for shopping and taking me to ballet lessons in Wilkes-Barre. Mr. Hess had a late model, spring green Buick with large tail fins. My mother bought new furniture for the big house, and Mr. Hess had a special red recliner that was designated exclusively for his use.

Mom organized a summer garden party and invited all of our friends and relatives. There were more than a hundred people on the sprawling lawn and enough food to feed two hundred!

After a few months on the market, a newlywed couple, from Pittston, decided to purchase our cottage, and gave my parents a deposit. On Christmas Eve, a few weeks before the scheduled closing, the young man was killed instantly when an automobile lift collapsed on him. My parents were then faced with the continued expense of managing two homes, which they could not afford. In the dead of winter, we moved back across the street with all of the new furniture, including Mr. Hess's recliner which now bore an oval shape on the back cushion from his bald head.

Since the purchase of the larger house across the street had fallen through, my parents began a total renovation of our existing home, starting with replacement of the BrickTex faux brick asphalt exterior with new aluminum siding. My father found a way to complete every project that Mom desired, from new plaster walls and a crystal chandelier, to glass sliding doors and a sundeck. He performed all of the labor himself, in the evening, after returning from work. My parents decided to trade the antique organ for knotty pine paneling on the front porch. We had always loved looking at the moon and stars with the German telescope that Dad brought home from the war, but when Lynne wanted to play the piano, my father traded the telescope for an upright grand. The piano was secured on the back of a borrowed pick-up truck. As Lynne and I watched from behind our white picket fence, Dad turned toward the driveway and the piano fell off onto Route 92, shattering into a million resounding pieces.

In addition to the cottages and farms, many residents of Harding lived in single wide trailers. Emma's Trailer Court, located along the river, five miles north of our house, had more than fifty trailers tethered to concrete pads located adjacent to "Emma's on the Trail" seafood restaurant. My best friend, from first through fourth grades, Mary Collins, lived in a trailer on a plot of open farmland far from the trailer court. We rode our bikes and climbed trees along the dirt roads that surrounded the farmland. When we felt brave, we peddled down Della Jane Lane to stare at Della Jane's house in the hope of seeing her. She was a very old woman with long white hair who lived in a house without electricity or any modern conveniences.

In the summer of 1965, my father bought and installed an above-ground swimming pool in our backyard. We jumped, swam and played in that pool all day, every day, never complaining of boredom. If I wasn't sitting high in a tree when my mother called me in for dinner, I was in the pool. One afternoon, I was still swimming when she called me to the supper table from the window upstairs. As I threw my leg over the three foot high, narrow pool edge, my foot slipped on the liner. I felt the center rim rip into my groin and fell onto the lawn in dizzying pain. Moments later, I heard my mother calling me for dinner, again, as I tried to get up and walk. I could not walk and, as I lay there bleeding, my father appeared and carried me upstairs.

I begged my parents not to call the doctor, insisting that I would not let him look at me "there," but within a short time, Dr. Testa arrived, carrying his medical bag. He asked my mother to prepare her bed for an examination by lining it with newspaper to absorb the blood. By that time, the injury had caused enormous swelling and the examination was quick. I was instructed to get dressed as Dr. Testa held a private meeting with my parents. He informed them that, unfortunately, my hymen had been ruptured, but I was expected to make a full recovery. Not another word was ever mentioned about the accident. The following weekend, my father began construction on an in-ground concrete pool.

Lynne and I were inseparable, exploring the idyllic countryside on our bicycles, picking blackberries along the riverbank, and playing softball in the field behind our house. In the winter, we couldn't wait for snow days to sled down the hills surrounding our house, and ice skate on the pond at night. Traveling in the back of Dad's enormous Buick, we pretended to be housewives, like Mom, with me as "Mrs. Palm Springs" and Lynne as "Mrs. Palm." When we arrived at our relatives' homes in Connecticut for summer visits, we imagined ourselves as Jackie Kennedy, staying at fancy hotels with our handsome, rich husbands.

In reality, as a nervous, pre-pubescent ten-year-old, I bit my fingernails down to the quick, so severely, in fact, that there was blood encrusted around the cuticles. I had a habit tick that involved licking the tips of my fingers by constantly alternating hands in my mouth. To complete the package, I had a speech impediment that resulted in the letters "G," "J" and the "Ch" combination forming a spit-filled sound as my back teeth closed tightly, thereby filling my mouth with saliva. "Church" was particularly horrendous. Twice a week, I was pulled out of class and sent to the nurse's office for speech lessons.

Every Easter, my Grandmother Irene took Lynne and me to Kresge's, in Pittston, for live, dyed peeps. There were hundreds of colored peeps in sectioned wooden crates in the back of the store and we were allowed to choose the color then bond with the baby chick throughout the High Holy season. Although the peeps did not live very long, the one my grandmother bought me in 1965 did quite well for a period of time.

Grandma Irene lived with us from Thanksgiving to late spring because there was no central heating system in her company mining house; a coal fired stove in the kitchen was the only source of heat. I had chosen a blue peep that Easter and she was still growing strong when it was time for Grandma to go back home, so the chick went with her and lived in the garden outside her front door.

Lynne developed allergies and was being seen by a pediatrician in Wilkes-Barre. One early summer day, my parents dropped me off at Grandma's while they took Lynne to her doctor's appointment. Grandma received a phone call, from relatives in Connecticut, who said that they were coming to visit her the next day. She told me that her guests were worthy of a very special dinner and, since she didn't have the heart to slaughter "Blue," we were going to take her to town and trade the live chicken for a dead one. I was consumed with horror.

My grandmother was about four feet ten inches tall, completely round in stature, with braided white hair, bowed legs and one tooth. I had to accompany her to town, on a public bus, with a live, blue-tipped feathered chicken flapping its wings in a brown paper bag. It was beyond a cringe-worthy experience.

The very next day there was a table covered with a fine linen tablecloth, set up outside under the peach tree, and Grandma served her guests fresh roasted chicken with all of the trimmings. It was a splendid feast.

Except for Dad's constant reminder that we were poor and Mother's mantra that "we are rich in spirit," I didn't feel poor or different. We seemed to have everything we needed for a happy life, including a swimming pool and summer vacations at the seashore.

Chapter Five

"What you have to do is work with the raw material you have, namely you, and never let up."
-Helen Gurley Brown

When I began fifth grade at Harding Elementary, a new girl showed up in our class. Marcy Schiffman lived in a large home on the river and had been transferred to the country school when all of the small, local schools merged into one large district, and she was no longer permitted to attend school in town.

The moment Marcy was introduced to our class by the fifth grade teacher, Mr. Sharobba, my entire life changed. The foundation of my happiness crumbled as the veil of innocence was lifted. Marcy looked different from any girl my age that I had ever seen and, in that instant, came the realization that I was different.

Marcy's light brown, shoulder length hair was clean, shiny and straight, parted to the side and fastened with a long barrette. She wore a white cotton blouse with a button-down collar and a wool herringbone skirt. The outfit was completed with dark knee socks and leather penny loafers. She looked as if she had just stepped out of the pages of my mother's *Spiegel* catalog. From that day forward, fashion became my goal for popularity in school.

Marcy became my best friend and she introduced me to a strange, new world that I had never imagined. My new state of being included boys, clothes, makeup and music. Marcy's parents welcomed me into their home and once a week they invited me to join them for dinner at Percy Brown's cafeteria in downtown Wilkes-Barre. On Saturdays, Marcy and I took the bus from Pittston to Wilkes-Barre, to shop at Kresge's for cosmetics, and then to look at clothes in the Teen Shoppe.

Marcy's father owned the Boston Shoe Store, on Main Street in Pittston, where her mother also worked full-time. When the store closed at six o'clock in the evening, the Schiffmans often enjoyed dinner at Fox Hill Country Club where they were active golf members. Mr. and Mrs. Schiffman each had their own Cadillacs and they employed a woman to care for their three children and provide light housekeeping duties.

On my first visit to Kresge's, Marcy took me into the make-up department and suggested that we buy frosted white lipstick. The model on the lipstick package was stunning, and I told Marcy that I wanted to look just like her. "That's my cousin, Colleen Corby," Marcy explained. "She and her sister are both models in New York City." "Well," I said, "Look! She's wearing a lot more than lipstick! I want to buy everything." I spent every penny in my purse to complete the look, which included Cover Girl Medicated Foundation, Coty cornflower blue eye shadow, Maybelline black mascara and Tangee white frosted lipstick. I bought a small mirror and applied all of the makeup on the bus ride back to Pittston. When Mrs. Schiffman dropped me off at home that evening, I carefully snuck through the living room and went straight to the bathroom to wash my face. I knew that my father wouldn't approve of my new look – but I loved it!

I began buying *Glamour* and *Cosmopolitan* regularly at Dymond's Store, and I read every word, from cover to cover. Gloria Steinem's essays and Helen Gurley Brown's editorials were like words of wisdom from sophisticated older sisters. Every month, it felt as if the pair snuggled up next to me when I sat down and opened the magazines, whispering their wonderful advice in my ears. In addition to valuable advice, I also learned the names of popular clothing labels, such as Bobbie Brooks and Villager, and I became determined to acquire the clothes and shoes required for my new look. I applied for a job at Rosenthals, the teen shop next door to the Boston Shoe Store; I was hired to work Thursday nights and Saturdays. I spent my entire paycheck on clothes and felt amazing when I bought my first Bobbie Brooks outfit – cream colored wide bell bottom pants with a sleeveless striped sweater vest and solid turtleneck. My transformation was complete…or so I thought.

One day, Marcy gently commented that the rather large cavity in my bottom front tooth needed to be fixed. She said that there was a dentist right across the street from her father's store. She was certain he could perform the necessary work for a reasonable price. By now, my mother had taken a part-time job as a cook in a nursing home, five days a week, working from two o'clock in the afternoon until seven o'clock in the evening. The extra income had eased the financial burden of raising two teenage daughters on my father's modest income as a diesel mechanic. I discussed the dentist bill with my parents and they agreed to pay for the repair.

Marcy and I were inseparable but as different as night and day. We planned our outfits for the Friday night football games, went "down the riverbank" with the boys at half-time, and kept our promises to not "go all the way." When Marcy was dining at the country club with her parents, I was heating up the dinner Mom had left for us before going to work. After school, Marcy went to her parent's store to do homework, while my sister and I went home to an empty house. Often, on Saturday evenings, I was invited to join Marcy's family for services at Temple B'nai Brith.

In 1967, the Shirtz family sold their home and we had new next door neighbors. The Cervuti family moved in. Mr. Cervuti came home from work around four o'clock in the afternoon and started drinking beer. A few hours later, he could be heard screaming obscenities at his wife and two daughters. My parents had to call the police more than a few times because Mr. Cervuti was allegedly hitting his wife and she was crying for help. One day after school, their sixteen-year-old daughter called me over to her porch and handed me a paperback book. She said that I would love reading it but that I should keep the book a secret. When I got back to my bedroom and began reading, I was shocked; it was a book of lesbian pornography. I hid it under my pajamas in a dresser drawer.

I began sneaking cigarettes from my father's Lucky Strike pack, as well as from my mother's Parliaments which she kept hidden in her lingerie drawer. Every night, when Dad went to pick Mom up from work, I went outside, either behind the house or down by the riverbank, to smoke my cigarette. Betty Jane Schiffman, Marcy's mother, smoked too, but Marcy never touched a cigarette.

Three of Mom's four sisters smoked. I loved the raucous laughter when they visited us in the summer. Wearing tight skirts and stiletto heels, the women took long, deliberate drags on their cigarettes as they sat around the kitchen table, smoke billowing below the florescent light fixture, telling stories of their latest escapades. Two of my aunts had been married a total of eight times.

When I was fourteen, I convinced my parents to sign working papers which would allow me to accept a job at the party favor factory. I finally had enough money to become a regular Marlboro smoker. While I was working after school from three o'clock in the afternoon to seven o'clock in the evening, Marcy was practicing to join the cheerleading squad. Her circle of friends expanded after she made the team, and it now included the best-dressed, most popular girls in school. Girls like me, from blue-collar families, were called "greasers." Like the character Rizzo in *Grease*, I only appeared to be tough when, in fact, I was simply a little rough around the edges.

My sixteenth birthday was a defining moment. It liberated me from life in the country. I passed my driver's license test on the first attempt, driving my cousin's 1971 red Chevy Corvair convertible. My father paid $16.00, at a junkyard, for a 1961 Chevy Impala. He rebuilt the engine and, with the compressor he had in our basement, painted the car navy blue – my favorite color. On the driver's door, just above the handle, he monogrammed my initials in gold. I was free to cruise! I never took the school bus again or had to ask for a ride to work. I drove my grandmother home after Sunday dinner, took my mother and sister shopping at the mall, and cruised up and down Wyoming Avenue on Saturday nights. In 1972, I began driving to Wilkes-Barre to attend the Marilyn Gauntlett Modeling and Finishing School.

By the spring of 1973, the modeling agency began sending me out on small promotional jobs such as Grant's new store opening in the Pittston Plaza. The owner received positive feedback and decided to book me for a few runway fashion shows. I weighed ninety pounds and stood 5 feet 4 inches, so the clothes fit me perfectly. In what seemed like no time, I was booked for two shows every week at local department stores, and my photograph often appeared in local newspapers. From time to time, when Mrs. Gauntlett was unavailable, she asked me to serve as a fashion show commentator.

A few weeks before my high school graduation, I received a phone call from Mrs. Gauntlett who told me that I'd been requested to audition for a very promising opportunity. When I arrived, models were lined up from the agency door all the way down the hallway to the elevator. A catwalk was set up in one of the agency's rooms for girls to walk up and back in front of a group of six men, after which we were dismissed. The next day, Mrs. Gauntlett called with the exciting news that I had been chosen, as one of three girls, to serve as Miss Pocono International Raceway for the Winston Cup Pocono 500 race in June. I rode in the back of a convertible with Richard Petty, waving to fans as we drove around the racetrack. Throughout the two-day event, I was given VIP status and greeted many guests and celebrity drivers. My parents were ecstatic!

Chapter Six

"A man likes to sleep with a brainy girl.
She's a challenge. If he makes good with her,
he figures he must be good himself."
-Helen Gurley Brown

"A liberated woman is one who has sex before
marriage and a job after."
-Gloria Steinem

Upon graduating from high school, the party favor factory owner offered me a full-time position as a floor lady. I graciously declined the opportunity, explaining that I had always dreamed of working as a secretary. The state employment agency helped me to find a clerical position at Atlas Chain and Cable Company, in West Pittston, where I met the most beautiful, sophisticated woman I had ever seen. JoAnn Castellino was the executive secretary to Don Walsh, the president of Atlas Chain. She had been the first runner up in the Miss Pennsylvania contest, graduated from a private women's college, and had worked as an airline stewardess before marrying her husband, an attorney from a prominent Pittston family.

In training me to use the massive switchboard so that I could cover her lunch hours, JoAnn had a profound influence on my speech and diction. Her voluptuous lips formed words perfectly, each syllable clearly enunciated and without a trace of geographic colloquialism. In other words, the familiar "coal cracker" accent and phrases, which identify many residents of The Valley, were undetectable. She was sexy without trying and she exuded self-confidence. I decided that JoAnn was the type of woman I wished to become.

Although JoAnn was ten years my senior, we quickly became close friends. She invited me to her apartment for lunch and introduced me to her husband, Joe, and encouraged me to accompany the group for dinner at night when the office staff went to a bar to unwind. I told her all about my boyfriend, Angelo "Ang" Falzone, a sophomore at Temple University, who had been captain of the Wyoming Area football team.

During my senior year, I focused on work and modeling school and did not get serious with anyone. I made plans to attend the senior prom with a good friend but, just two weeks before the event, he reconciled with a former girlfriend and I was left without a date. My sister Lynne's friend, Joanne Falzone, said, "I'll bet my brother Angelo would take you to the prom. You're pretty and he just broke up with his girlfriend of four years." Ang was a perfect gentleman and our friendship evolved into a serious affair over the summer.

I explained to Ang that I had never "done it" with another boy and he promised that, when we agreed the time was right, he would be gentle and extremely careful. On a steamy night in July, we drove to his parent's summer home, along the Susquehanna River, where Ang parked his father's white Lincoln Continental behind the barn. We were both surprised that none of the expected bleeding had occurred and that intercourse had not been painful. I did not know at the time that Ang thought I had lied about being a virgin. The memory of the swimming pool accident years earlier never even occurred to me.

JoAnn asked if I had been intimate with Ang and I confessed my secret. Ang was the first boy that I "went all the way" with, in the back seat of his father's Lincoln Continental, just two weeks prior. JoAnn was quick to ask if I was on "the pill" and, when I admitted that I was not, but that we had been careful, she made arrangements with her gynecologist. She accompanied me to my first appointment with Dr. Giovannini who confirmed that I was not pregnant and gave me a prescription for birth control pills. We continued our romance for several months before deciding it was time to go our separate ways as friends.

With the introduction of the birth control pill in 1960, women were liberated from the expectation that marriage and motherhood were their prescribed fate. They could engage in sexual relations, freely, without the fear of an unwanted pregnancy. However, as historians Ellen Carol DuBois and Lynn Dumenil state, *"the ethic of sexual liberation set different sorts of restraints on women. What sexual liberation meant before women's liberation is captured in images of women in miniskirts and go-go boots, with exaggerated eye makeup and long straight hair, signaling their availability to men. Women were not supposed to be sexual adventurers themselves so much as rewards for the men who crashed through the barricades of respectability."*[8]

There had been other boys in my life, of course, and I had learned the technical details regarding human sexuality in health class but, in the only conversation my mother had with me about sex, she stated firmly, "No one will want you if you're used! Girls who have sex before marriage are whores!" It had been my decision to remain firm in abstaining from intercourse while I was in high school; I did not want to be one of the girls who got "knocked up" and had to leave school.

My first real boyfriend, Frank Goryl, taught me how to kiss when I was fourteen. Victor "Butchy" Bosco was next and, since he had a car, things got a little hotter. When I decided to break up with Butchy, after two years of dating, my mother said, "If you break up with him, you will never bring another boy into this house!" My father responded with, "Helen, my God, she's only sixteen!"

My job at Atlas Chain had become the perfect start to a secretarial career and I loved it. JoAnn asked me to join her in serving on the credit union board of directors. Soon thereafter, the board selected me to represent the company in the Miss Credit Union contest where I was chosen as the first runner up. The contest was broadcast on a local AM radio station and my parents listened intently as I answered each question correctly, thereby eliminating the other contestants until there were only two of us remaining. When the final question was asked, my opponent stumbled and gave an incomplete response. I completed the answer correctly but the contest organizer, my opponent's uncle, quickly declared her the winner. Shocked listeners complained to their credit union officers and, after twenty years of success, the contest was discontinued.

Later that summer, Mrs. Gauntlett suggested that I audition with Mr. Johnson, the vice-president of women's fashion at Hess's department store in Allentown. Hess's was famous for their fashion show in the restaurant, every Saturday, featuring read-to-wear and couture. When I mentioned to JoAnn that I had an interview at Hess's, she suggested that I make a day of it by having dinner with her brother-in-law, Frank, at Lehigh University in Bethlehem.

I arrived at Lehigh early, after being informed on the spot, by Mr. Johnson, that I wasn't tall enough to join his team. Frank's friends, at the Delta Phi fraternity house, told me that I would find him in the gym, where he was packing a parachute. When I entered the gym, Frank, whom I had met briefly once before, quickly apologized for his appearance, stating that he had expected to see me at the house. He had been practicing packing his parachute for a timed test that would determine his acceptance on the Lehigh skydiving team. We walked back to the fraternity house together where Frank introduced me to his friends, who kept me company while he got ready for dinner.

The fraternity house was quite impressive with art and architecture that was unfamiliar to me including a grand piano in the living room. A formally dressed chef introduced herself and offered refreshments. The atmosphere was elegant with a sense of history that I felt for the first time. It was a different world, and I wanted it to be my world.

I continued to follow the advice of Helen Gurley Brown and the politics of Gloria Steinem. I embraced the women's liberation movement with passion and a firm commitment to become an independent career girl. Gurley Brown and "the pill" gave me permission to enjoy sex. A woman's orgasm, she suggested, was equally as important as pleasing your man, which was very important. *Cosmopolitan* offered advice on both, and I was a serious student determined to learn.

Shortly after we met, Frank began commuting from Bethlehem, Pennsylvania to Harding so that we could spend time together. Frank respected and shared my feminist ideology. He understood my career aspirations, the desire to expand my intellectual and social horizons beyond living in The Valley, and my commitment to remaining single and childless. At the beginning of Frank's final semester at Lehigh, I reminded him and my parents that I was moving to south Florida, as I had planned after vacationing there for two consecutive summers. Frank responded immediately, pleading, "Please don't move without me. I'll be graduating in December and we can move there together. If you leave me now, I'll flunk out. Please."

Although we had a very serious relationship, I was surprised by Frank's response. He had been accepted to law school in Washington, D.C., beginning in the fall of 1975. We discussed our plans further, and decided to live together in Fort Lauderdale for six months before he had to move on with his plans. I was completely stunned when Frank proposed to me at my parent's anniversary dinner party in September. He had sold his BMW motorcycle, a gift from his parents for making the Dean's List, to buy my engagement ring. When he presented the ring, he said, "We don't need a date for the wedding. I just want you to know that I'm crazy in love with you, and I want us to be together forever." My parents were over the moon; Frank's parents were completely disgusted.

In December I told my parents that I'd given notice to my boss at Atlas Chain, telling him of my plans to move to Florida. My mother was quick to state, "So, you're moving to Florida and Frank is moving to Florida and you expect me to believe that you're going to live separately? I'm telling you right now, Nancy, that if you and Frank plan to disgrace this family by shacking up, I will disown you and you will never be allowed back in this house! DO YOU UNDERSTAND ME?"

In *Revolution from Within: A Book of Self Esteem*, Gloria Steinem states that she and her girlfriends dreamed of escaping their working-class Toledo neighborhood and that if she had written a book about that period of time it would have been titled *Getting Out. "Our dreams of escape from the neighborhood kept us from focusing on our probable fates as lifetime factory workers who rebelled only on weekends, or homemakers who played pinochle, went bowling, and sometimes got a beating on Saturday nights."* Steinem explains that, for girls, show business was the only way to avoid such a fate as she recalls the success of singer Teresa Brewer who had won the "Ted Mack Amateur Hour" while still in high school, and never returned to Toledo.[9]

I trembled at the choices before me, unable to imagine either being estranged from my family or not living with Frank. Frank's proposed solution did nothing to calm me. "So, let's get married before we move to Florida. We've already decided that we want to be together forever. Nothing will change, I promise. I love you."

I had begun packing for the Florida move when my father took my arm firmly and said, "Nancy, you don't have to do this. You're just a little girl." Later that week, I received a phone call at work from Dr. Jerry Rosenstein, a close friend of Frank's brother, Joe, and his sister-in-law, JoAnn. We had dined with Jerry a few times. He said that he liked me and did not intend to insult me but had heard that we were planning to get married. "Nancy, the Castellinos are really upset about this wedding," he stated. "Your level of education is far beneath Frank's and the odds of this relationship working are very slim. Please reconsider. I've already spoken to Frank."

Frank had attended Scranton Preparatory School before transferring to Pittston Area High School, in his senior year, to join the wrestling team. He was the class valedictorian, spoke fluent French, and played classical piano. His personality was congenial; he was brilliant, kind, loving and an Al Pacino look-alike. By marrying me, he offered me a hand up but never, ever suggested it. In fact, he treated me as his full equal, as though we were the same, but I always knew we were different.

I was nineteen when we were married on February 15, 1975. With only three weeks' notice, my mother planned a wedding for two hundred and fifty invited guests. The formal ceremony took place at the Second Presbyterian Church. The next day, we began the twenty-four hour drive to Fort Lauderdale to start our new lives together.

Chapter Seven

"The art of life is not controlling what happens to us, but using what happens to us."
-Gloria Steinem

"Life is uncharted territory, It reveals its story one moment at a time."
-Dr. Leo Buscaglia

We arrived in Hollywood on February 17th, after driving for more than twenty-four hours. It was high season in Florida, and every hotel and motel was sold out along the Gold Coast. When we showed up at the front desk of a Howard Johnson's motel at 2:00 a.m., feeling dirty and exhausted, we were given permission to sleep in our car in the covered parking garage.

My cousin Charlotte's family had been in the construction and real estate business in south Florida since the late 1950's. She had a two-bedroom, two bath rental apartment on Hollywood Boulevard that happened to be vacant, and later that morning, we rented it from her. The next day, Charlotte invited us to her home for a dinner party to welcome us to Florida and celebrate our marriage. Grandma Irene's oldest daughter, Mary, was my cousin Charlotte's mother. Aunt Mary had been living in Florida for more than twenty years and she had married a total of five times; one of her husbands, she'd married twice. Aunt Mary worked as a waitress until 1956, when she and her second husband, Gus, opened a restaurant near Fort Lauderdale.

Aunt Mary was thrilled that we had decided to live in Florida. Her love and generosity gave us a wonderful sense of family. This was the first time I had lived away from my family and the adjustment was difficult. For several weeks, I called my parents every night, drank too much wine, and cried myself to sleep. I was determined, however, to transform my dream of becoming a successful career woman into a reality.

Two days after arriving in Hollywood, Frank and I visited an employment agency together. I interviewed for a clerical position at an insurance agency a mile from our apartment. Frank interviewed with the Diplomat Hotel, on Hollywood Beach, for a position as assistant controller. Frank majored in mathematics at Lehigh University and he had graduated with a degree in economics. We were both awarded the positions we interviewed for and we began work the following week.

The Diplomat Hotel gave us the wonderful opportunity to assist with events outside of the normal work schedule, in exchange for meeting performers and enjoying their shows. We met Olivia Newton John, Telly Savalas, and Jackie Gleason. We formed many new friendships and, in a short time, felt comfortable calling south Florida our home. We had rented the apartment for six months when Frank suggested that we consider buying a home to build equity. I was quick to state that I had no desire to live in the suburbs in a traditional home, but that I would consider a condo. Frank felt that a house would be a better investment, and since he was an accountant, I agreed. He informed his parents of our plan, and they immediately sent a check for $10,000 toward the down payment. We bought a small, fully furnished home in Pembroke Pines for $39,900. The house had a large back yard, and a week later we brought home a shaggy rescue dog and named him Ralph.

Before long I became restless and bored at work in the small insurance agency cubicle. My daydreams led me to a daily reading of the *Miami Herald* classifieds and I decided to challenge myself. I replied to an ad for a legal assistant at a large defense firm on Flagler Street and was granted an interview. Miami was at least an hour commute from Pembroke Pines during rush hour traffic. At that point in time, there were racial tensions and bombings in certain areas, making it a potentially dangerous drive, but I was offered the job at a salary that was beyond my wildest dreams. Within six months, I was promoted to a paralegal position, and began earning more money than my husband.

Frank had decided months before that he did not want to attend law school, and instead he had pursued his C.P.A. accreditation. He accepted a position at Cherry, Bekaert and Holland, an accounting firm in North Miami Beach. We were doing well financially, and enjoyed traveling back home to Pennsylvania several times a year. We also traveled to Vermont for skiing in February. One of Frank's clients, the controller of Caterpillar Tractor, in Nassau, Bahamas, invited me to accompany Frank on his business trips several times a year, giving me the opportunity to experience new friendships in a different culture.

By then, my sister Lynne, whose friendship I missed terribly, was a junior in high school, and I was earning enough money to provide her with new clothes for every special occasion. We also sent her plane tickets and encouraged her to spend a few weeks with us several times a year. During one visit, Lynne confided that it often felt as if someone had died since I left home. A particular sadness seemed to hang in the air. I sent my parents plane tickets and they enjoyed their first flight together for a one week vacation. When I drove them to the Miami Airport for their return flight to Pennsylvania, my father wiped a tear from his eye. I had never seen him cry, and I realized at that moment, that he missed me terribly, much more than I had ever imagined.

I loved my position with Corlett, Merritt, Killian and Sikes, one of Miami's most prestigious defense law firms, but felt it was time to check out the area's opportunities for part-time modeling jobs. One Saturday morning, I interviewed with the owner of the Cover Girl Modeling Agency, who asked me to provide headshots and stroll the catwalk. She immediately proclaimed that I was too short for the runway and had a nose that was too big for photography. The words, "too short" and "big nose" stung. I was hired a few times for public relations gigs such as new car dealership grand openings, but I put away any further thoughts regarding modeling, and focused on my legal career, thinking *at least I'm smart*!

In June 1976, we flew home to Pennsylvania for Lynne's high school graduation. When I approached baggage claim and did not see my father, I instantly knew that something was wrong. Frank's parents were there to pick us up and share the devastating news that my father had suffered a massive heart attack. They brought us directly to the hospital where Dad was in intensive care. We extended our stay for another week until my father was discharged and settled comfortably at home. We had a house and friends in Florida as well as good paying jobs that we loved. I was not ready to return to Pennsylvania permanently. Frank suggested that we take our time to decide but that he would support whatever my heart desired.

My father recovered and returned to work, but two years later, while driving home one afternoon, he had another heart attack. I knew, without a doubt, that it was time to return to Pennsylvania. We began sending resumes and listed our house with a local real estate agent. In 1979 we packed up our car, rented our furnished house to the listing agent, and drove straight through the night, with Ralph curled up in the backseat. I started crying when we closed the door to our home in Pembroke Pines, and didn't stop until we reached Virginia. When we arrived at my parent's house, they were ecstatic and couldn't wait to tell us about the little house they had found for us to rent in West Wyoming.

Chapter Eight

"Happy or unhappy, families are all mysterious. We have only to imagine how differently we would be described – and will be, after our deaths – by each of the family members who believe they know us."

-Gloria Steinem

"Being human means you will make mistakes. And you will make mistakes, because failure is God's way of moving you in another direction."

-Oprah Winfrey

I was hired, within a week, as the executive secretary to Charles D. Flack Sr., the president of Diamond Manufacturing Company. My office was located one block from the house we had rented on Maple Street. Life was different in Pennsylvania. Instead of weekends at the beach, we visited our families for dinner, attended every holiday dinner – twice, once at the VanDermark's and, again, at the Castellino's. We were available when people needed us. In essence, there was less excitement but much deeper joy.

Grandma Irene was eighty-five and still living in her own home when we returned from Florida. She invited us for dinner often, until her health began to rapidly decline. She died in the spring of 1980. Shortly after my grandmother's death, we bought a house in Harding, five miles north of my parent's house. It was new construction in the Hex Acres development, built on land that had been a farm for more than a hundred years.

When Frank and I had been married for five years we began discussing the joys of parenthood. All of our friends were already having children. In December 1980, much to the shock of our close friends and family, I became pregnant. We decided that if our baby was a boy, we'd like to name him Peter Frank, but not until we discussed it with Frank's parents. They were touched and pleased by our decision.

The Castellinos had three sons, spaced five years apart. Joseph, the eldest, Peter, and my husband, Frank, the youngest. Peter Frank Castellino, their middle son, was five years older than Frank and five years younger than Joseph. A handsome boy, he held the power weightlifting titles for his weight class in Pennsylvania and was Mr. Atlantic Coast as well as an Olympic hopeful. He was on scholarship and in his freshman year at Hiram Scott College, in Scottsbluff, Nebraska, when, on an unusually warm day in May, he went swimming in Lake Alice with a group of his schoolmates. He swam out about 75 yards from shore, and it was thought that because he was so muscular and the water was so cold, he may have suffered cramps as he attempted to swim back. He was just 20 years old when he died. The school called his mother in the middle of the afternoon, and informed her of the accident by stating, "Mrs. Castellino, we believe your son drowned this morning. We'll let you know when we find the body." Eight agonizing hours later, the body was recovered. Frank's father and older brother flew to Nebraska to identify Peter's body and accompany him home. Mrs. Castellino never changed the calendar in her kitchen from May 16, 1966.

I loved *getting* pregnant and, much to everyone's surprise, I loved *being* pregnant! I took sewing lessons and made an entire wardrobe of maternity dresses with matching purses. I read every book available in our local library on natural childbirth and raising children. I did not smoke, drink alcohol or consume caffeine. I did, however, eat – a lot and, over the course of my pregnancy, gained sixty-five pounds! Frank and I attended Lamaze natural childbirth classes at the new Geisinger Medical Center, in Wilkes-Barre. Rusty Flack, my new boss at Diamond Manufacturing, offered to convert the company gym into a nursery if I would agree to return to work, but Frank and I had decided, together, that I would stay at home after the baby was born.

After twelve hours of labor, Peter Frank Castellino entered the world on August 28, 1981 at 7:52 p.m. When the doctor announced that I had given birth to a boy, I could hardly believe it! Peter was perfect in every way. I breastfed my baby for eighteen months, made all of his baby food, baked whole wheat bread every week and sang lullabies every night. I loved being Peter's mother more than anything in the world. A few months later, I became pregnant with our second child.

As a stay-at-home mother, I made friends in our family-friendly community. One afternoon, I glanced across the street and did a double-take. It was like a quick sighting of Jackie "O!" Irene Sisk's slender figure, elegant French twist and oversized sunglasses were a striking difference from the average Hex Acres housewife. I had been pushing Peter's baby carriage when we struck up a conversation.

Irene introduced herself and said that she had also recently met another one of our new neighbors who asked what she had been working on. When Irene responded that she was painting, the neighbor's reply indicated that she, too, assumed that Irene was a sophisticate. "Do you sell your work?" the neighbor asked. "Oh no, of course not!" Irene giggled, "It's a bathroom wall!"

Irene and I began making regular dates for coffee, getting together in the late afternoon, before our husbands returned from work. Irene was in her late thirties, with a teenage son and daughter, when she surprised me one day with the announcement that she was pregnant. Her daughter, Leah, was born in 1982 and was introduced to Peter when they were both toddlers. They became close friends and playmates. Irene became the closest friend that I had made in many years. We shared everything together, from bedroom secrets to holiday recipes and how to get a child out of a tall tree. Irene's beauty and sophistication were only surpassed by the incredible warmth of her personality.

When I was eight months pregnant with our second child, I drove my parents to a wedding on Long Island where my sister had moved after her wedding. As we were traveling on Interstate 80 eastbound through New Jersey, I looked over at my father, sitting in the front passenger seat, and saw that he was perspiring profusely. He said, "I'm okay, Nancy. Don't worry about me. You sure are a good driver to manage this New York City traffic." When we arrived at my sister Lynne's house, two hours later, Dad asked for a cold ginger ale. His complexion was gray and we knew that something was seriously wrong. Lynne drove him to the Mather Hospital emergency room, in Port Jefferson, where he was stabilized and transferred by ambulance to Cornell University Medical Center.

The doctor, who had performed the first heart transplant in the United States, performed a heart catherization on my father and informed us that he had approximately three weeks to live. He said that my father was a perfect candidate for a heart transplant but, at sixty-five years of age, he was too old for the procedure. When I entered my father's hospital room, he said, "Nancy, I'm going to die and I want you to make sure that you get top dollar for my tools, especially the compressor in the basement. Your mother is going to need the money." Tears ran down my face as I said goodbye to my father and returned home to prepare for childbirth.

Two days later, my mother phoned to tell me that the doctor had visited my father and informed him that he had sent Dad's test results to a dynamic young heart surgeon at Mt. Sinai Medical Center, on Fifth Avenue, in Manhattan. Dr. Bruce Mindich said that he would be willing to perform bypass surgery on Dad, but that he wanted it to be clearly understood that my father had only a twenty-five percent chance of surviving the surgery. My father said, "I'm going to die anyway. Of course, I'll take the chance!" Dad was transferred to Mt. Sinai Medical Center immediately, and within two days, underwent open heart surgery.

My obstetrician, Dr. Chung, would not allow me to travel to New York for Dad's operation, so a good friend came to stay with me throughout the day. Dad went into the operating room at 6:00 a.m. and I finally received a phone call from my mother, at six o'clock that evening. "Your father survived the surgery," she said somberly, "but the doctor told me that the next twenty-four hours are critical. There is a very good chance that Dad will not make it." Frank fell asleep in the downstairs den that night, and I went to bed, exhausted, at around 10:00 p.m.

At two o'clock in the morning, the phone rang; I raced into the kitchen to answer it. At exactly the same time, Frank ran across the room to his desk and picked up the phone. Simultaneously, we heard the caller ask, "Is Emmit there?" I immediately replied, "I'm sorry, you must have the wrong number." The caller insisted, "May I please speak to Emmit?" There was static in the background making the call sound far away. "Who are you?" I asked. "I'm his mother. Is he okay?" At that point, Frank threw down the phone and ran upstairs where he found me startled. "Where are you calling from?" I asked. She replied, "Bloomsburg" and I told her that she had the wrong number. My grandmother, Emma Decker VanDermark, died in 1930 when my father was just thirteen years old. The phone call remains a mystery.

My father survived the operation and returned home two weeks later, a week before his second grandchild was born.

Helena Lynne Castellino, named to honor my mother, Helen, was born on September 28, 1983 at 10:58 a.m. When Dr. Chung announced that I had given birth to a girl, I was thrilled! Helena was perfect in every way and our family was complete.

When I took Helena for her six week checkup, the doctor detected a heart disorder and ordered further testing at Geisinger's main facility in Danville, Pennsylvania. She was diagnosed with a ventricular septal defect. The American Heart Association explains it this way; "*VSD* is a hole in the wall separating the two lower chambers of the heart. In normal development, the wall between the chambers closes before the fetus is born, so that by birth, oxygen-rich blood is kept from mixing with the oxygen-poor blood." Helena's condition was closely monitored by pediatric cardiologists for the next year and a half before she was discharged. The small hole had closed and surgery was not required.

Peter and Helena were inseparable. When Peter imagined himself as Batman, he declared that Helena was Robin as she stood by his side waiting to take direction. Peter potty-trained his sister when she was eighteen months old by repeatedly taking her into the bathroom and telling her to stand there and watch.

Our home in the country provided an idyllic setting for the children to play outside, climbing trees and fences, riding bikes and swimming in our neighbor Irene's pool all summer. I planted roses, gladiolas, cannas and tiger lilies along the post and rail fence that surrounded our half-acre property.

My children were my passion. I joyfully exhausted all of my energy on their care and that of our comfortable country home. I often obsessed about the children's health. I felt that this life was too good to be true. I once called the pediatrician, Dr. Wolfe, expressing my concern that Peter might have an ingrown toenail. He annoyingly said that it could wait for his next office visit. On another occasion, I called Dr. Wolfe to confess that I had fed the children canned chicken soup after which he replied "Mrs. Castellino, that's quite alright as long as you haven't fed them the can!"

When Peter was three years old, he developed asthma and was treated with a nebulizer each night before bed. There were nights, when he had a cold and simply could not stop coughing, that I had to take him to the emergency room. There were also many times when I had to hold Peter upright in a chair for most of the night until the coughing stopped, which left both of us exhausted.

I felt that I was a good wife. I worked out three times a week at aerobics classes in town and I had returned to my pre-pregnancy weight by the time Helena was two. I looked and felt sexy, but by the time I got to bed at night, all I really wanted to do was sleep. I never admitted to my husband, family or friends that I felt seriously sleep deprived. Sex, as frequently as Frank enjoyed it, had become more of an obligation than a pleasurable experience for me. Since I erroneously thought that, as far as Frank was concerned, sex was the most important aspect of our marriage, I tried to hide my disinterest, but my lack of passion had seriously impacted our relationship.

I felt incredibly disappointed that I was unable to please the man that I loved so deeply. I remembered thinking that my passionate love for the children and dedication to the well-being of our family, along with what was most definitely mutually satisfying sex, was enough for my happiness. I began to feel that, in my role as a wife, I was inadequate and had become a failure.

I enrolled the children at Apple Tree Nursery and Primary School in Kingston, three days a week and took a part-time position with an assistant district attorney. I worked hours that corresponded precisely with the children's school schedule and hired a housekeeper to help at home. Frank and I began to socialize more often, enjoying neighborhood parties, as well as classical concerts at the Northeastern Pennsylvania Philharmonic. From all appearances, we looked like a perfectly happy family. In reality, the stress and strain had begun to affect our marriage. I was no longer afraid that Frank would find a girlfriend to satisfy him. Instead, I wished that he had one!

As tensions between us escalated, I felt the bonds of our marriage begin to fray. The criticism of a devoted husband who adored me became my most difficult personal challenge. While Frank maintained the character of a good and faithful man, I was so fixated on my children that I failed to remember that my husband needed my attention as well.

When I boarded an early morning bus headed to New York City in January 1988, I did not feel lovely…but I wanted to. So, I employed the tactic that had worked effectively when I took the bus to Kresge's in Wilkes-Barre two decades earlier. I piled on the makeup, faux accessories, and Dior coat acquired on credit. I asked my husband for $100 and went to the cosmetics department at Saks Fifth Avenue to boost my self- esteem…temporarily.

Chapter Nine

"Something very beautiful happens to people
when their world has fallen apart:
a humility, a nobility, a higher intelligence
emerges at just the point when our
knees hit the floor."

-Marianne Williamson

June 8, 1988

It was a glorious late spring morning when the children and I drove to Kingston for their last day at the Apple Tree School before the summer break. Peter's frequent colds and ear infections had established a new normal, in terms of his general health, with amoxycillin often prescribed every month. With the sunroof open, we sang oldies on the drive along the Susquehanna as Peter took a break between verses to cough. I dropped the children off for end of the year classroom festivities and continued on to work.

Later that day, I greeted Peter and Helena at the door when they arrived at home, anxious to hear about the fun. Helena showed me the trinkets in her purse that she had collected from her nursery school friends and teachers. Peter was unusually quiet and, when I asked about the field trip to the ice cream parlor, he replied that his legs hurt on the walk. It was Wednesday and we always had dinner at Frank's parent's house so I suggested a rest for Peter after another dose of cough medicine.

Grandma Josephine had prepared a wonderful Italian dinner, served in the formal dining room, but Peter did not eat anything, including his dessert. When it was time to leave, he said, "Mom, could I ride in your car, please?" Frank had met us in town after work and Helena was happy for the opportunity to ride "shotgun" in her father's car. Peter pulled the seatbelt across his neck and cried, "Ouch, that hurt!" I reached over and felt that the glands just below his ears were swollen. As soon as we got home, I called Dr. Landau, our pediatrician.

"Oh, don't worry," said Dr. Landau. "He probably has mono and I can check him out in the morning. It's that time of year." I was very worried and pleaded, "Please, Dr. Landau, can you see him tonight?" Dr. Landau knew Peter well as a patient and his daughter, Maya, was Peter's classmate at the Apple Tree School. "Of course. Bring him to the Nesbitt Hospital emergency room. I'll meet you there." We left the house immediately after I kissed Helena goodnight. As we traveled Route 92, past my parent's house, Peter said, "Mom, you are the best mother God ever made." My intuition told me that something terrible was happening.

After a brief examination, Dr. Landau said, "Mrs. Castellino, I don't even know how to tell you this. Peter is a very sick young man. I'm calling in a pediatric oncologist." Frightened and confused, I asked, "What do you mean 'very sick'? What is a pediatric oncologist?" I did not want to hear his answer. I wanted to stay calm for Peter but when I heard the word "cancer," I began to sob. "Cancer! What are you talking about? I don't understand. Peter was in school today. How could he have cancer?"

I called Frank and asked him to get to the hospital quickly because Peter was very sick. I did not say the word "cancer." I called my neighbor and best friend, Irene, to inform her of the situation and ask her to look after Helena. She said, "Nancy, calm down. You're so neurotic about the kids. I'm sure he'll be fine."

By the time Frank had arrived, Peter had been given a room. We had informed the doctors that we wanted to take our son to the best hospital in the world. Frank's brother, Joe, was present in the room with us when the ambulance arrived to transport Peter to Children's Hospital of Philadelphia, two hours away. A private duty nurse was assigned to ride in the ambulance with us; Frank followed behind in his car. We were only thirty minutes into the trip when both of Peter's eyes hemorrhaged, the whites filling up with blood. I screamed, "Oh my God!" What is happening to my son?" It was only the beginning of the horror.

The ambulance pulled into a covered area, the back doors were flung open and Peter was rushed out from the stretcher he had been lying on, to a gurney surrounded by medical personnel. I ran behind them as they pushed through large double doors and quickly got ahead of me. Within seconds, Peter was gone and I was escorted into a waiting area where, a few minutes later, Frank joined me. Later that morning, Frank and I were taken to a conference room where a team of doctors were assembled to speak with us.

"We are very sorry but your son is seriously ill," explained one of the doctors. "Peter has leukemia. Acute lymphoblastic leukemia, to be exact. We call it ALL." Tears streaming down my face, I pleaded, "Please, just tell me he's going to be alright and that he'll climb trees again and get into trouble at school." Another doctor replied, "We can't promise you anything. Let me explain. This is a type of cancer where the bone marrow makes too many immature white blood cells. The average child has between 5,000 and 10,000 white blood cells. Peter's blood test shows that he has a white blood cell count of 395,000 and it's doubling every twelve hours." From across the long table, another doctor said, "It's the third highest white count ever diagnosed at Children's Hospital. The other two children did not live past three weeks."

Massive doses of chemotherapy were begun immediately and Peter was admitted to the Intensive Care Unit. As I sat next to his bed, an oncology nurse explained that Children's Hospital of Philadelphia, known better by its acronym CHOP, is a teaching hospital. Therefore, Peter's treatment protocol, the chemotherapy plan that would be administered, was determined by the flip of a coin, selected randomly, not specifically, based upon his clinical diagnosis. She informed me that Peter would be receiving a protocol developed in Germany that prescribes so much intravenous chemotherapy to be administered that it brings the child very close to death. The next seventy-two hours were critical and, if he survived this period, he'd have a chance to live. However, his overall prognosis, without this treatment, was less than two months. Over and over, in my mind, I heard *death*...less than two months...*death*. Two nurses found me in the ladies room, on the floor, sobbing. When they lifted me up, I begged them to awaken me from this nightmare.

I sat next to Peter's bed in the ICU for three days without leaving the hospital. The doctors were incredibly kind showing me where their locker room was located so that I could shower, and explaining everything that was happening. Peter responded to the chemotherapy as we had hoped and went into remission immediately. On the morning of the fourth day, he was moved into a room where another child was a patient in the adjacent bed. She was a beautiful, three-year-old girl who was being treated for neuroblastoma, a type of cancer that forms in nerve tissue. My eyes were slits, swollen from crying, and causing me to look deformed. I did not want to be rude but was unable to speak with the child's family members who were present in the room. The girl's mother came over, put her arms around me and offered a prayer of comfort from the Quran. The next day, her child died while undergoing surgery.

Frank had been commuting between Philadelphia and Harding. He spent a little time with Helena and a few hours catching up at his office. When Frank returned to Philadelphia, with a change of clothes and a yellow rose for me, we cried together. Peter consoled us by saying that we shouldn't worry; he was going to be just fine. The oncology nurses said that if Peter continued to respond well to the treatment, we would be allowed to check in to the Ronald McDonald House on Chestnut Street and return, daily, for outpatient intravenous chemotherapy. A social worker presented us with a few pamphlets written to prepare for the challenges ahead. One brochure offered suggestions regarding how to discuss the possibility of death with a child. It explained that the pediatric patient should distribute his cherished personal items to loved ones as the end of life approached. The nightmare was becoming much darker.

We checked into the Ronald McDonald House as a family; Peter had been discharged after nearly two weeks as an inpatient, and Frank brought Helena to Philadelphia. The staff was incredibly accommodating and went out of their way to make sure we were comfortable and had everything we needed. They gave us a large suite of rooms on the third floor with a private bathroom. We were given a tour of the sparkling commercial kitchen and invited to prepare our favorite meals while meeting other resident families. It was a relief for us to be together but none of this felt good. There was nothing that anyone could do or say that mattered to me. I was waiting for someone to tell me that this was a mistake. This happened to other people's children, not mine. This happened to the strong mothers, not me. I could not imagine burying my son. I thought about what would happen to Helena if I accompanied Peter to his grave. The pain was unbearable. My thoughts were torturous.

At the beginning of August, in the sweltering city heat, Peter began radiation treatments at the University of Pennsylvania Hospital. First, he was permanently tattooed in the areas where the radiation would be targeted: his head and lower back. Ninety-five percent of his body was cancerous, including his brain and spinal cord. Then, we were introduced to the radiologist and his team who explained that Peter would receive the highest possible level of radiation. Combined with his chemotherapy, this treatment could cause serious side effects including learning disabilities, as well as sight and hearing problems. Peter had scored in the 95th percentile on standardized testing in first grade. I cried out, "How could this be happening to my perfect little boy?" as the doctor directed his final statement to Peter. "Now, Peter, I want you to understand that every Friday is Hawaiian shirt day here, so I'm ordering you to get a sharp looking one!" The next day, Peter began his radiation treatments.

A representative from the Starlight Foundation approached us in the waiting room at CHOP. She said that Peter could choose any wish that he would like fulfilled and, after he had decided, we should contact her. In that moment, I realized that Peter was dying.

Peter spoke directly with the Starlight Foundation representative, telling her that he would like, more than anything in the whole world, to see the volcanoes in Hawaii. Perhaps this desire, which was new to me, was precipitated by radiation shirt day but it wasn't the only unusual wish. Peter was requesting strange foods that he had never tasted prior to receiving chemotherapy or radiation. One morning, he asked for a bagel with cream cheese and the hospital staff was happy to fulfill his wish.

The Starlight Foundation was too, and within a few weeks, we were on a plane to Oahu. The Foundation provided funding for every expense, from round-trip airline tickets for our family, hotel rooms, three meals a day, and money for excursions so that Peter could see everything his heart desired. One day, we flew to the Big Island where there was an active volcano. The tour bus drove us up as close as possible where we saw steam coming out of the ground. On the return trip, Peter yelled, "The volcano is erupting!" The bus driver pulled over to the side of the road and, sure enough, red hot lava was spewing from the top. The tour guide said it was a very rare occurrence and I was grateful that Peter's wish was fulfilled.

Peter was unable to return to second grade for the opening of the school year. He was becoming increasingly ill as a side effect of the treatment and his immune system was unable to fight off even the slightest infection. The nursing staff, at CHOP, taught me how to calculate his immune level factor by using blood count numbers factored into a mathematical equation. If the number was too low, we had to keep Peter away from friends and family until he regained his strength. Sometime in September, Peter's thick, brown hair began falling out. One morning, he called me into his room and showed me the pillow. I gasped when I saw the chunks, not strands, of hair that had fallen out. I ran my fingers through his hair and began to cry. Once again, Peter consoled me by telling me it was alright, he would grow new hair. Within three days, he was completely bald, his skin was gray, and he looked like he was dying.

When his blood counts stabilized, the doctors gave Peter permission to attend school. His teacher arranged a meeting with the parents of his classmates in order for me to explain the seriousness of Peter's condition and so that they could prepare the children for his appearance. On his first day back to Apple Tree, Peter put on one of his Little League baseball caps to cover his bald head and walked into the school, excited to be back with his friends. I felt as though my heart would break when I thought about the challenge he was facing and I prayed that he would find strength. At the end of the school day, I went into Peter's classroom for a status report and found him playing with classmates. The teacher said that he had only worn the baseball cap for a little while before removing it and announcing to the class that he was going to be the next president of the Hair Club for Men!

Peter began receiving his intravenous chemotherapy treatments at Mercy Hospital in Wilkes-Barre under the direction of Dwaraki Penugonda, M.D., Pediatrics. It was enough medicine to keep him in remission, and unfortunately, prevent any new hair from growing. We sat patiently as Peter received the prescribed dose and then pulled the car to the roadside as he vomited his guts up all the way home. By the time we pulled into the driveway, he was ready to run around outside and play.

Every month, we drove to Philadelphia where Peter had a spinal tap procedure to determine whether or not the cancer had returned. It was an extremely painful procedure and difficult for us to watch him endure. Helena stayed by his side as Dr. Belasco placed the foot long needle into his spine, with Frank grasping his hand tightly, as a bone marrow sample was extracted. His little sister never missed supporting him through a procedure and he depended upon her constant presence.

The stress and strain on my thirteen year marriage was complicated by my loss of perspective and complete lack of long-term vision for our future. All that I could think of was how to manage day by day, sometimes hour to hour, with a seriously ill son, a little girl who was internalizing intense emotions, and a husband who expected the kind of intimacy that I was incapable of providing.

I incessantly visualized Peter's funeral. I did not want to share my time or attention with Frank. As my family suffered, every resentment that I harbored through the years festered like an open wound. Inconsequential, small irritations became major obstacles to overcome as the threads that bound us in love began to fray. I thought that if this challenge was the crushing end of my family and our dreams, I wanted to spend it alone with Peter and Helena.

I still loved Frank and continued to think of him as my soulmate forever, but I wanted to end our marriage. I needed a place to ease the tension and free myself from caring for anyone but my children. I was spinning out of control, losing not only my mind but, ultimately, my husband and home. I was on a path of self-destruction, through deconstruction, that disguised itself as the road to autonomy.

Throughout the winter, Peter often spiked fevers over 100 degrees, which meant an immediate hospitalization. In the middle of the night, I took him to the hospital where he was admitted as an inpatient for several days. During his first year of chemotherapy, Peter received countless blood and platelet transfusions. It was the height of the AIDS crisis and I pleaded with the doctors to give him my blood. They explained that I was the number one candidate in the event that Peter required a bone marrow transplant and, if they gave him my blood, he would never be able to receive my bone marrow. In the spring of 1989, when chickenpox spread throughout the school, Peter was confined to home for several weeks. I met with his teachers and we kept up with his schoolwork at home.

Our divorce was finalized in May. Frank and I agreed to joint custody of the children. I refused any child support, insisting that I would get a job that covered all of our expenses. I signed over our house to Frank for $1.00 at a meeting with his lawyer who promptly replied that I had just become the best ex-wife in Luzerne County history. I packed my clothes and personal items into my small BMW and moved into an apartment in town.

I was hired immediately, by Michael Cefalo, a prominent West Pittston lawyer. He accommodated my schedule with the children by allowing me to begin work at six o'clock in the morning, when the children were with Frank, and leave at two o'clock in the afternoon. When Peter and Helena were with me, I dropped them off at school and Frank picked them up. If Peter was unable to attend school, I stayed with him at Frank's house. We worked seamlessly as a team to protect our beloved children from any further heartache, and for a while, they felt as though they had two loving homes.

A week after my divorce, I drove by my parent's house on my way to Frank's to pick up the children. I saw my father outside watering his flower garden and stopped for a quick visit. Dad was happy to see me and invited me inside for a cup of coffee. My father's black lung disease had progressed and he was using oxygen most of the day. After a few minutes, I said that I had to leave but Dad said that he wished I would slow down and find more time to visit. In reality, my parents were devastated by my divorce. They missed our family dinners and were concerned about the change they observed in me and the toll that Peter's illness was taking. I kissed my parents goodbye and drove five miles north along the river.

As I was greeting the children and Frank, the phone rang. I couldn't hear what Frank was saying but I saw the concerned look on his face as he hung up. My father had collapsed moments after I drove away from his house…the ambulance was on the way. I jumped into my car and sped along the two-lane road, arriving in time to see Dad lying on the bedroom floor, paramedics attempting to resuscitate him. I followed the ambulance to Nesbitt Hospital where my father was pronounced dead. An orderly escorted me into an examining room where my father's lifeless body lay on a gurney, Mother at his side. I held his warm, rough hands for the last time and said goodbye.

Within a period of eleven months, my son was diagnosed with cancer, Frank and I divorced after thirteen years of marriage, and I lost my beloved father and the home I had shared with my family.

Chapter Ten

"A miracle is a reasonable thing to ask for."
-Marianne Williamson

"No storm lasts forever."
-Dr. Wayne Dyer

With Helena, Frank, and I present at his side for every treatment, Peter continued to manage chemotherapy well. There were frightening episodes of fevers that required hospitalizations, a seriously compromised immune system, and platelet transfusions, but we learned to adjust to rapid changes in his condition. We were a broken family, traveling on shaky ground in uncharted territory. We were existing moment to moment and yet it felt as if the Universe was strengthening us. People everywhere offered their heartfelt assistance. Family members, friends, employers, medical personnel, even the local media supported us. Through every step of our journey into hell, someone stepped forward to hold a candle and help light the way during the darkest of nights.

By 1991, Helena was enjoying new friendships, both at school and in her dance classes. Peter joined the basketball team and continued with Little League. The joint custody arrangement was undoubtedly difficult for the children, but they never expressed any anger or frustration, either to Frank or me. Along with the challenges of junior high school, imagine packing all of your belongings every Saturday morning, moving to another residence, then repacking before school every Tuesday morning to move again. This went on fifty-two weeks a year for more than a decade. It would not be fair to Peter and Helena to understate the stress that our divorce placed upon their young, very complicated lives.

Frank remarried, and I took a chance on a job in radio sales, which eventually resulted in a significant increase in my income. We were also able to move into a larger house, one located within walking distance of the children's elementary school.

My new employer, WKRZ, is the number one contemporary hit radio station in northeastern Pennsylvania. Regardless of the station's ratings, selling air time, an intangible and expensive commodity, was a challenge. Every morning the sales team, led by the general manager, met in the conference room. The tone of the sales meetings typically depended upon the general manager's mood and the team's sales figures. I learned quickly that by calling on at least ten potential clients, I could reliably average at least one sale per day. I was energized by the challenge, and grateful for the opportunity.

One day the station's owner flew in on his Lear jet to lead the morning pep talk. He presented each one of us with a paperback book and said it had changed his life. He suggested that if we truly desired to become outstanding account executives, we needed to visualize our success as he had done, by reading the best-seller *You'll See It When* You *Believe It* by Dr. Wayne Dyer.

I stayed up all night reading Dyer's suggestions on how to dramatically alter our reality by changing our thoughts. On "transformation" Dyer writes:

There are no limits to your ability to think. You can imagine yourself doing anything...I am suggesting that you can experience a major portion of your life in this dimension of transcending your form, that is, in transformation.

...This is the place where you can not only live a miracle, but create miracles as well...By believing you are a soul with a body rather than a body with a soul. You will create for yourself a life that is literally without limitations. You will begin to see miracles occurring simply because you believe in them and expect them to materialize for you.[10]

Dyer claimed that we had the power to manifest everything from riches to complete healing from a serious illness, simply by changing the way we think about it. He wrote that even if no one had ever survived the diagnosis that one was facing, believing in one's radiant health held the possibility of creating it. *What if this is true?* I thought. *What if* it's *possible to heal oneself from cancer?* We had nothing to lose in radically altering our thought processes, and there was Dyer's own testimony, as well as that of the radio station owner, to back up their claim. I wanted to believe that it was possible for Peter to survive. I wanted to stop rehearsing his funeral. I wanted to visualize him driving a car, playing sports, attending high school…living and loving.

I didn't waste any time in sharing Dyer's modern-day philosophy with Peter. One night at dinner, he said, "Mom, if I do die from leukemia, it will be the greatest adventure ever!" In that moment, I realized that if I had never accomplished another thing in my life, I had been successful in removing the fear of death from my child. This was a defining moment and I was determined to become a student of Dyer's philosophy, studying cassette tapes by day, and books by night. Peter remained open-minded regarding the power of creative visualization, and there were countless people praying for Peter's healing.

Months went by without a single hospitalization or significant medical emergency. It was the first time in years that we had been liberated from the restrictions imposed by Peter's treatment. We had adjusted to home confinement in the spring when the annual chicken pox outbreak occurred. Peter had re-grown and lost his hair three more times. Each new crop of hair arrived thicker and curlier, before once again leaving him with a shiny bald head. At several different points during his treatment, the bottoms of his feet became covered with warts, making it extremely painful for him to walk and run. Every night I applied medicine to each sore, then covered his feet with white cotton socks before tucking him into bed. He never complained and no one ever knew about the warts except for the two of us and Helena.

A spirit of optimism permeated our home and we began to dream. Helena, who had become a wonderful ballet and jazz dancer, decided that she wanted to pursue acting. Peter was determined to become a member of the Wyoming Area Warrior football team. He asked Dr. Belasco, his pediatric oncologist, at every visit, if he could play football, and her answer was always the same, "Your bones are too brittle from the chemotherapy, Peter. We'll see how it goes."

I left the radio station for a senior account executive position at Cable One, a Williamsport based advertising company, with all of the rights for commercial advertising on the Turner Broadcasting Networks, including CNN. My territory included all of northeastern Pennsylvania, the Pocono mountains, and Sussex County, New Jersey.

When the Gulf War catapulted CNN into the mainstream, with live coverage of the conflict available twenty-four hours a day, I sold out every available commercial advertising space, in every geographical territory, and on every single network. Since these were local advertisers, for whom television advertising had not previously been feasible, they were thrilled to view their own commercials on TV, hear feedback from customers, and see an immediate increase in sales and store traffic. Within a short time, I had become the second top producing sales person in the company, and my confidence was soaring. Our little family was no longer in crisis-management mode, existing from day to day, in fear of the future. We planned, dreamed, and lived, as if tomorrow really did exist.

Chapter Eleven

"The more you see yourself as what you'd like to become, and act as if what you want is already there, the more you'll activate those dormant forces that will collaborate to transform your dream into your reality."
-Dr. Wayne Dyer

I gave myself the freedom to dream again. I maintained a positive outlook and was taking better care of my body by running three miles every morning before work. After dinner, I worked out at the Pittston YMCA for half an hour, and took five mile bike rides on the weekends. I felt it was time to resurrect a dream that had been buried for more than twenty years. I had headshots taken by a professional photographer and hired an employment agency to write and design my resume. I visualized myself working for one of the only two companies in the world that would fulfill my heart's desire to work in the fashion industry, Chanel and Dior. These were the only two resumes that I submitted, and both companies offered me a job.

I accepted the position offered by Christian Dior Parfums, as a freelance skin care model and assistant account executive. The terms of my employment included the promise of a salaried position as an account executive, once I had gained hands-on experience by working in department stores for a minimum of six months. Bill Ticho, my new boss, offered me $500 a week and reimbursement for gas and tolls. There were neither healthcare benefits nor job security, but I felt that the opportunity was worth the risk.

Dior sent me to Washington, D.C. for training with their most esteemed corporate educator, Colleen Sandler. Ms. Sandler exemplified the Dior image in both her striking physical beauty as well as her elegance. She grew up in Johannesburg, South Africa where her parents settled after fleeing Nazi Germany in the late 1930's. Colleen's father opened a jewelry store and the family enjoyed a cultured and refined lifestyle. During our extensive four-day training session, Colleen described every product in the extensive Christian Dior skincare line, in detail, captivating not only *me* with her mesmerizing British accent, but also every customer who visited us at the Bloomingdale's counter. In addition to traveling throughout the United States, as a member of Dior's training team, Ms. Sandler hosted amazing parties, on behalf of Dior, at the French Embassy.

I was assigned a territory that included eighty-five Bon Ton and Hess's department stores from Pittsburgh to Johnson City, New York. My responsibilities ranged from in-store events and new product launches, to hiring and training retail sales associates. I visited every store in my territory, personally met with store managers, and when overnights were required, I stayed at the Red Roof Inn for $26.00 a night in order to stay within my expense account budget. When staff in Dior's corporate office in New York City reviewed my expense report, they took note of the fact that I was staying in a modestly priced motel and I was immediately summoned to meet with the Philadelphia regional sales director.

Mary Martini Panvini had arrived at Penn Station, in Philadelphia, wearing a full-length mink coat, and accompanied by a representative from LVMH (Louis Vuitton, Moet, Hennessey) headquarters in Paris. She looked as if she had just stepped out of the pages of *Vogue;* I had never met anyone who exuded that amount of pure glamour and striking beauty. She welcomed me as a member of her team with incredible warmth, offered her support, and encouraged my recommendations. Mary said that she had already received positive feedback about me from department stores that had never expected to receive a personal visit from a representative of Dior. She also delivered an important message; hereafter, as a member of the Dior sales team, whenever I traveled on company business, I would be expected to stay at luxury class Ritz Carlton Hotels instead of family oriented motels!

One September morning I traveled to Johnson City, New York for a meeting with the Dior counter manager at the Bon Ton, but upon my arrival I was informed that she had called in sick. With my morning plans cancelled, I decided to visit a nearby salon to have my hair done.

While waiting for the stylist, I picked up a copy of the local newspaper and noticed an article announcing that Dr. Wayne Dyer would be speaking at the State University of New York (SUNY) campus on November 1st. I called the box office and was told that the first three rows had already been reserved for a group of local nuns, so I purchased the first ticket, fourth row center. When I arrived home that afternoon, I excitedly announced to the children that I was going to hear Dr. Wayne Dyer speak in person; they were thrilled.

In October, during a visit to the Bon Ton headquarters in York, Pennsylvania, the transmission suddenly seized up on my car and it stopped on Interstate 81. The mechanic at the shop where the car had been towed, informed me that a new transmission would cost me $3,000, and since I was $2,900 short, I left the car to be junked. Happily, fate intervened. Later on that evening, a friend from the local radio station, the well-known disc jockey Jumpin' Jeff Walker, offered to loan me an old Jaguar that he had sitting in his driveway. "The only problem with it, Nancy," he explained, "is that if you don't keep the hood tied down with a rope, it will fly up over the windshield. Other than that," he continued with a laugh, "it drives pretty well and you can keep it as long as you need to." The loaner vehicle was a life-saver, and I arranged my schedule to visit stores within a close radius to home while I began saving money for a down payment on another car.

As the date for the Dyer lecture approached, I knew that it would be impossible to drive the old Jaguar all the way from West Pittston, Pennsylvania to Johnson City, New York, so I announced to the children that I would not be attending. "But Mom," Peter anguished, "you have to find a way to get there. He's your favorite guy in the whole world." Peter and Helena had spent several years listening to Dyer's voice on cassette tapes every time they got into my car. "I can't trust Jeff's car to get me to New York," I said, shaking my head. "I'm just grateful that the old Jaguar is getting me to work every day."

A week later, I was called into New York for a meeting with Dior's vice president of sales, Mark Scott, and the New York regional sales director, Susan Nappa. We met at the Essex House Hotel on Central

Park. Mr. Scott thanked me for arriving from northeastern Pennsylvania, promptly at nine o'clock in the morning, and then said that he wanted to share news of an important development. Bill Ticho had decided to retire and Mr. Scott offered me a promotion to account executive. "Nancy, you would be a wonderful asset to our sales team," Mark said, "and I hope you will take this position. I've restructured the territory to include all of Pennsylvania, southern New Jersey, upstate New York, Baltimore and Washington, D.C."

My heart sank into my stomach as I realized that it would be impossible to manage this vast geographical expanse while raising two children in northeastern Pennsylvania. "Thank you for considering me, Mark," I replied, "but I live near Scranton with my two children, and I just don't think this is feasible." Mark quickly pulled an index card out of his lapel pocket and said, "Sure, you can do it, Nancy. Look, I've drawn a map on this card. You're here in Scranton, right in the middle of the territory, with just about every store in a two hour radius from home. We are including a company car, an American Express expense account, full benefits, and three assistants with your package."

Oh, how I wanted it, but quickly replied, "Washington, D.C.? That's at least four hours away and I'm at home for dinner with my children every night. Thank you, but I just can't accept it." I got up from the table, expressed my appreciation, and left the restaurant. I was walking to the parking garage on 57th Street when I heard Susan Nappa calling me from behind. "Nancy, wait, please! You're perfect for this position and it's perfect for you. This is everything you've dreamed about and worked hard for. We will help you to make this work. I want you on my team. Please come back and let's talk about the details." I returned to the table with Susan and Mark, explained that my children are my priority, without exception, and agreed to give this amazing opportunity every ounce of career energy and commitment to success possible.

On November 1st, I drove to the Dyer lecture in my brand new car as Peter and Helena waved goodbye from the driveway. I took my place behind three rows of nuns and felt chills run through my body when

Dr. Dyer walked out onto the stage. I was mesmerized by every word as he walked back and forth speaking for over an hour, without notes, before breaking for intermission. I purchased his latest book and stood in line to have it signed. "Dr. Dyer," I said, "I can never, ever thank you enough for your life-changing work. It has helped to save my son's life and change mine forever."

Dyer asked me to step out of the long line that had formed for book signings. "How?" he asked. "What do you mean in saying that my work has helped to save your son's life?" In as few words as possible I explained to Dr. Dyer that Peter had been diagnosed with leukemia and spent several years on chemotherapy. I told him that I had dreaded the constant thoughts of Peter's funeral that flooded my mind and that we were now thriving beyond all of our expectations. Dr. Dyer said, "Nancy, will you join me on the stage tonight and share your story with the three thousand people who are out there in the audience?" I said that it would be an honor.

That evening I walked out onto the stage, after being introduced by Dr. Dyer, and said, "If I had known that Dr. Wayne Dyer was going to invite me to speak to three thousand people on the stage tonight, I would NOT have worn see-through pants!" After the audience expressed their amusement, I continued in a more serious vein. "What I am about to tell you is completely unrehearsed. It is a story of hope."

After the lecture, throngs of people lined up to speak with me and share their stories of cancer, healing and inspiration. I left my contact information with Dr. Dyer's assistant, Maya, but did not expect to hear from him. A few weeks later, I was staying at the Ritz Carlton Hotel in Tyson's Corner, a suburb of Washington, D.C., when I received a cell phone call from a woman in Pennsylvania. Sue Kenely said that she was Dr. Dyer's booking agent. Dr. Dyer had mentioned that he thought the two of us would get along well, and since she lived less than an hour from me in Pennsylvania, he'd suggested that Sue give me a call to introduce herself. Toward that end, he had shared my phone number with her. Sue and I agreed to meet for dinner in Allentown, and when we did, we were delighted to learn that Wayne was absolutely right. We had much in common, including the fact that we were both single.

Although Frank and I shared joint custody of Peter and Helena, there were no strict guidelines regarding our arrangement. If Frank and his wife wanted to travel or had plans, I would keep the children with me and adjust my work schedule accordingly. Frank reciprocated whenever I had plans of my own. I arranged my schedule to be out of town, overnight, every Monday so that I could visit my farthest accounts early in the week. I also planned to visit my Washington, D.C. accounts on Saturdays, thereby allowing me to take the children to the Ritz Carlton on Fridays, after school, once a month. The Ritz staff quickly made themselves familiar with Peter and Helena, upgrading us to the concierge level, and offering a limousine while I was at work.

Dr. Dyer's booking agent, Sue Kenely, invited me to assist her throughout the northeast, with every Dyer lecture she had booked. We picked Wayne and his assistant, Maya, up at the airport, in a rented Lincoln Town car, then checked into the hotel and set up the auditorium for the lecture. Maya, Sue and I enjoyed dinner together and Wayne often joined us to share an O'Doul's and a vegetarian meal. We shared stories about the challenges of raising teenage children, and over time, became good friends. While I lavished Wayne with Dior products for his wife Marcy, and for their daughters, he supplied me with guidance and inspiration. I often asked him to elaborate further on a particular story that I found interesting or perplexing. Wayne encouraged me to read and study his source material including the great philosophers whose work he quoted. I had never heard of Tolstoy or Maslow, Jung or Frankl, but I was an eager student. I asked about the Unity Church that Wayne mentioned in one of his books. He said that he often lectured at Unity and that it was a non-denominational organization devoted to teaching metaphysics and inspiring people to live fearlessly.

I found a Unity Church in Wilkes-Barre, located in a building that it shared with a homeless shelter. The minister, Reverend Ann Marie Acacio, was radiant as she welcomed visitors for Sunday morning services and metaphysics classes throughout the week. Reverend Acacio exemplified the self-actualized, empowered woman I sought to become. She is a highly intelligent, master teacher whose spiritual guidance gave me wings.

I was captivated by the Unity bookstore where I became familiar with self-help authors whose work was entirely new to me. Marianne Williamson's *A Return to Love*, based upon *A Course in Miracles*, the deeply psychological work of William Thetford, made sense to me, and I related intimately to Williamson's personal anecdotes. Williamson's book *Illuminata* ended with a prayer in which she asked God to help us "find our way home, from the pain to peace, from fear to love, from hell to Heaven." It became the foundation of my own deepest prayers.

Chapter Twelve

"Education is the key to unlocking the world, a passport to freedom."

-Oprah Winfrey

I had been in a Dior sales meeting at our office overlooking Central Park, when my colleagues began speaking about their educational backgrounds. Everyone was shocked to discover that I was the only individual on the executive sales team without a college education. In fact, it was later brought to my attention that no one, in the history of the Dior sales team, had ever been hired without having at least some college.

I spent the following weekend researching college opportunities that would accommodate my children and career. The next really big dream began to form when I discovered that Smith College, Gloria Steinem's alma mater, had a program for non-traditional students whose opportunity for higher education had been interrupted by real life.

The Ada Comstock Scholars Program offered women the full experience of attending college, from living in a dorm and serving on the student council, to becoming a member of the crew team. *Wow*, I thought, *how I would love this program*! There were, however, two major drawbacks. The first was a requirement for prerequisite college course work that equaled a minimum of sixty credits. The second was that students had to take classes on the Smith College campus in Northampton, Massachusetts – five hours from my home.

Through further research, I learned that Vermont College, in Montpelier, offered a low-residency (aka limited-residency) program, available to qualified applicants without prior college credit. Students were required to take classes on campus for ten days, twice a year, while completing the required course work from home under the supervision of a professor whom the student chose while on campus. I considered the idea that if I devoted my two weeks' vacation time to an academic pursuit, it would be feasible for me to attend. I prepared my application immediately and was accepted for a residency which began in January, a few months later.

Peter and Helena shared my enthusiasm for the course of study that I had chosen carefully with input from my professor, Michelle Levitt. Ms. Levitt, a former Boston criminal attorney, became a poet, playwright and author by giving up her law practice to bartend while writing. The focus of my six month semester had been to write about female survivors of the Holocaust and African American women's biographies. I became deeply absorbed in stories of strength and survival. On a monthly business trip to Washington, D.C. with the children, we visited the Holocaust museum and were left speechless during the entire four hour drive home. When the horror of genocide settled into our consciousness, we spoke for days about the profound effects of the exhibits and video presentations.

I enthusiastically shared new information with Peter and Helena regularly through conversations and by wallpapering the back of our bathroom door with quotes from women whose work I was studying. They learned about Anne Frank, Maya Angelou, Miep Gies and Zora Neale Hurston while I had them on the toilet as a captive audience.

There was still time in my busy schedule to attend Dr. Wayne Dyer's seminars with Sue Kenely. I helped Wayne's trusted assistant, Maya, by recommending books to ticket holders before, during, and after every lecture. Many times, people who had seen Wayne on PBS or listened to his tapes, asked if I was his wife Marcy, but I was always quick to reply that Dr. Dyer was way more inspiring to me than any husband had been! In reality, there were countless events that led to me being alone in Wayne's hotel room where we sat talking about children and work. Wayne never expressed an iota of interest in me, nor I him, except for our friendship. One night, at dinner with Sue and Maya, Wayne stopped by our table and said, out of the blue, "You know, Nancy, what you need is a strong, powerful son-of-a-bitch in your life!" I was surprised and shocked by the comment, nevertheless, I thought about it from time to time, wondering how that son-of-a-bitch would conduct himself, and pondered why Wayne thought that I needed such a man to enhance my life.

Spiritual studies and Vermont College coursework were completed simultaneously and my life felt rich and fulfilling. After I completed twenty teaching credits in metaphysics, the Unity Church requested that I become a member of the board of directors. Reverend Ann Marie Acacio invited me to speak on occasional Sunday mornings and recommended me to the Unity congregation, in Johnson City, New York, where I delivered brief lectures based upon Dyer's work and its impact on my life.

Concurrently, the retail environment changed dramatically in the mid-1990's when computerized inventory tracking systems were installed in every department store. Gone were the days when an account executive visited a store, and together with the counter manager, planned events and ordered an ample quantity of merchandise to fulfill customer demands. For example, a store had at least twelve pieces of a best-selling lipstick on hand at all times, but when a special event was planned, additional quantities were shipped in to support the increased demand. The new computerized system, only allowed for multiples of three pieces based upon regular sales; any extra merchandise needed the approval of the department store's corporate office. Sales plummeted and it became necessary for Dior to streamline their sales staff. Several of my colleagues had lost their jobs and I was sure that my position was the next to be eliminated. Although my boss, Susan Nappa, reassured me, I felt that my lack of seniority was the biggest obstacle to keeping my job.

I no longer reverted to nervously anticipating the worst case scenario. Instead, I knew that it was time to proactively seek my next career move. I had heard that Mary Panvini, my former boss, had accepted a position as the vice president of Adrien Arpel Cosmetics. I distinctly remember driving home one day hoping that Mary would contact me and visualizing the call. As I pulled up in front of our house, Mary called, saying "Nancy, I'm running Adrien Arpel and I want you on my team. Please come in to New York and talk to me."

In 1959, eighteen year old Adrienne Newman (Née Joachim) a/k/a Adrien Arpel, took $400 she had earned from babysitting and launched what would eventually become a multi-million dollar business devoted to women's skin care. She became president of Adrien Arpel, Inc., an enterprise that included 500 salons across the United States and Canada.

I arrived at Adrien Arpel headquarters, on Fifth Avenue and 56th Street, for my interview with Mary Panvini. The receptionist escorted me into her office and Mary, looking more gorgeous than ever, greeted me warmly with a hug. She was wearing a black St. John knit suit with a double strand of pearls. Mary's hair was long and curly and her skin glowed radiantly. It was impossible to guess her age.

Mary Panvini had grown up in a working class family in south Philadelphia. As a young teenager, she took an interest in etiquette and won a table-setting contest at the John Wanamaker department store, where she was offered a part-time job. She later became an Estée Lauder counter manager at Wanamaker's in Philadelphia, and after being noticed by a Lauder corporate executive for her outstanding sales figures as well as her striking beauty, she was offered a position as an account executive for the Philadelphia territory. After several successful years with Lauder, Mary was hired by Christian Dior Parfums as their Philadelphia regional sales director.

Mary's husband, Vincent Panvini, was the Director of Government Affairs for the AFL-CIO in Washington, D.C. The couple had a condominium in Watergate Towers and a lovely home in Moorestown, New Jersey, a Philadelphia suburb. Vincent's high profile position afforded the couple opportunities for an unusually active social life, and friendships with notable politicians, including President Bill Clinton and First Lady Hillary Rodham Clinton. They dined at the White House often, and because of her work with Dior, also spent considerable time at the French Embassy where Mary organized lavish parties.

During my interview, Mary explained that Adrien Newman, who used the company's trade name of Adrien Arpel, had a contract dispute with the board of directors, and subsequently, spun off a new company, *Signature Club "A"* to sell her products on the Home Shopping

Network (HSN). As a result, the Adrien Arpel company was in a downward spiral. The company had a significant department store presence, including the entire mezzanine level at Bloomingdale's 59th Street, but they were now without a spokesperson at the helm. Arpel needed to secure their existing business and open new accounts to stabilize the manufacturing end of the operation to the satisfaction of the board of directors. Mary did not hold back from telling me that it was an extremely challenging opportunity, but she said she was prepared to offer me a generous salary and benefits package along with a company car. She said, "Nancy, I am prepared to make you the company's national training director. You will have the entire United States and Canada as your territories, and it will catapult your career in the cosmetics industry to the top. Please help me to make this company a success and I promise to reward you beyond your dreams!"

I accepted the Arpel position much to the dismay of my bosses and colleagues at Dior. Susan Nappa, who had been exceptionally supportive of my career and family life, said that my fears had been unfounded, and that I would never, ever have lost my job at Dior. "Nancy," Susan said angrily, "You do the work of two account executives. We would never have let you go! I can't believe you're going to work for Mary."

My first order of business was to visit the existing accounts and reassure store managers and employees that Adrien Arpel was getting back on track and we would soon be launching new products to add to our skincare and makeup collections. I held training seminars throughout the country, and organized special events in key stores, such as Bloomingdale's flagship 59th Street location, and Kaufman's headquarters in Pittsburgh. Our next priority was to find a new department store chain that would give the company a significant financial boost. Mary arranged meetings with the vice presidents of cosmetics at J.C. Penneys, in Plano, Texas and Sears, at their headquarters in Chicago.

Money at Adrien Arpel was much tighter than I had anticipated and, when we checked into our hotel in Texas, I was shocked to find that

Mary had only booked one room. There were two double beds, but there I was, for the first time in my life, sleeping with my boss! At dinner, Mary said that she and Vince had a friend that they would like to introduce me to. She described him as a prominent politician, and explained that they felt very strongly that Senator Bob Kerry would absolutely fall in love with me! I was cautiously interested and explained to Mary that my children and career were more than enough to handle. The following night, after our presentation with Penney's went smoothly, Vince Panvini called to say that he had spoken to Senator Kerry and a dinner party would be arranged.

A week later, we flew to Chicago to make our presentation to Sears. As I buckled my seatbelt for take-off, Mary took out a copy of the latest *Washington* magazine which featured Senator Bob Kerry on the cover. She stood up, in the aisle, and announced that I was going to be the First Lady of the United States when Senator Kerry married me and became President. She said, in her south Philadelphia style, "Look at her! Doesn't she look like First Lady material?" I flushed with embarrassment but understood that Mary meant well.

The Sears meeting was an outstanding success. The company's executives agreed to open three hundred and eighty-five stores as an initial roll out, with the promise of a thousand more at a later date. We arrived back at the New York office with our exciting news and the feeling that we had triumphed over a seriously adverse situation. The board of directors agreed, and decided unanimously to give up on their search for a celebrity spokesperson to represent the company. Instead, they named *me* as the new Adrien Arpel spokesperson.

Chapter Thirteen

"Where there is no struggle, there is no strength."
-Oprah Winfrey

"You'll see it...when you believe it."
-Dr. Wayne Dyer

At the same time, I was completing one semester at Vermont College and scheduled to begin another. My proposed travel schedule felt overwhelming, and I decided to take a leave of absence from school until I was confident in my new position. I explained, in a letter to my professor, Michelle Leavitt, that I had accepted a promotion at Adrien Arpel and needed six months off. When I returned to Montpelier to complete my study, Michelle said, "Nancy, you have to read Myrlie Evers Williams memoir, *Watch Me Fly*. I'm sure she mentioned Adrien Arpel in the book." *What?* I asked myself. I thought she had to be mistaken, but I went to the campus library, found the book and devoured her story. Toward the end of the book, Ms. Williams explained that after her husband, civil rights activist, Medgar Evers, was brutally murdered, she accepted a position as the national spokeswoman for Adrien Arpel Cosmetics. I nearly fell of my chair. There I was passionately engaged in a biographical study of African American women while serving as the newly appointed national spokesperson for Adrien Arpel. It was, from my viewpoint, divinely ordained, perfect synchronicity.

Mary organized a fabulous party on Sunday, November 1, 1998, at Bloomingdale's 59th Street, in the Adrien Arpel Spa on the mezzanine. She ordered a photo session in the office for my headshots and sent me to the Frederic Fekkai Salon to have my hair done. Mary took out a full page ad in *The New York Times* Sunday Style Section announcing me as the company's new spokesperson, and inviting guests to attend our party. One of my photographs was used to make a wall mural in Bloomingdale's that was ten feet high by twelve feet wide. Another photograph was used to make an ektachrome that was installed in every department store which carried Arpel throughout the United States and Canada. In my hometown, Boscov's stores in Scranton, at the Steamtown Mall, and in Wilkes-Barre, featured an Arpel ektachrome at the entrance to the cosmetics department. Mary took ads out in every major newspaper in the United States announcing my appointment. It was a fabulously exciting time that had, as Mary promised, exceeded my wildest dreams.

Arpel's catalog producer, Len Merullo, organized a catalog photo shoot in Branford, Connecticut on the Long Island Sound. We spent the day together, taking hundreds of photographs for our spring catalog. On the drive back to my car, in Danbury, Len asked if I was married and I replied that I was too busy for romance. He asked me to consider meeting his friend, Jay Shaw, former president of men's wear for Palm Beach, Inc. on a blind date, and I promised to think about it. Jay's management responsibilities had included Palm Beach Clothing, Gant, and Pierre Cardin.

A few weeks later, Mary called to inform me that a producer from the *Montel Williams Show* would be contacting me to schedule my appearance as a guest. I watched very little television and was unfamiliar with the show, but when the children arrived at home from school, they were ecstatic about the show. It was a segment focusing on the spread of germs and bacteria, through common items, such as groceries and makeup. I was featured as the Adrien Arpel spokesperson and a quasi-expert on bacteria in makeup. The audience watched in horror as a chemical substance was applied to various items, including packages of meat and mascara, that caused them to glow in the dark if bacteria was present. I discussed the time frame within which certain makeup items should be discarded. For example, many women keep their favorite lipstick tucked away in a handbag for years when it should be thrown away within a year. Mascara and other eye makeup products should be discarded every three months. Peter and Helena accompanied me to Montel's studio in New York and were treated royally by his staff in the green room. Life was sweet and wonderful.

Peter had completed six years of chemotherapy in 1994 and his doctor explained that he could not be declared "cured" until he was five years away from his last treatment. By 1998, we felt confident that Peter's health would continue to improve. Peter was a junior in high school and a member of the National Honor Society. He continued to plead with Dr. Belasco, at Children's Hospital of Philadelphia, for permission to join the high school football team. Helena was involved with a serious dance company and she remained focused on a creative path with her mind set on acting.

By winter, Peter decided that he wanted to run the San Diego Rock-n-Roll Marathon and raise $5,000 for the Leukemia and Lymphoma Society. I suggested that we speak with his doctors at Children's Hospital Of Philadelphia before he became too involved, but he was determined. Peter reassured me that if he had a chance to raise the money, he would be careful not to stress his body, even if it meant that he had to finish the marathon by walking the remainder of the twenty-six plus miles.

Within a week, we had exceeded Peter's $5,000 fund-raising goal for the Leukemia and Lymphoma Society. Adrien Arpel not only contributed to Peter's sponsorship, but they also offered to pay the round-trip airfare so that Helena and I could travel to San Diego to cheer Peter on. Peter's father, Frank, and our extended families contributed generously, as did Attorney Joseph Quinn, Attorney Michael Cefalo, Rusty Flack, the president of Diamond Manufacturing Company, Congressman Rafael Musto and Falcone Beverage Distributors.

One night, I received a phone call from a doctor who had heard that Peter was about to begin training for the marathon. He advised me that Peter should not consider running 26.2 miles after six years of chemotherapy. My response was immediate and definite, "Doctor, thank you for your concern, but Peter is intelligent and determined. I will not tell him that there is anything that he cannot accomplish if he feels capable." In early spring, Peter was assigned a trainer who accompanied him on Saturday mornings around Lake Scranton.

In June of 1998, cancer survivor Peter Castellino ran the San Diego Rock-n-Roll Marathon with a time of 5 hours and 9 minutes. His participation raised $5,000 in support of the Leukemia and Lymphoma Society.

It was around the time Peter had been training for the marathon that my mother had traveled to Florida for a well-deserved vacation from her job as a cook for six nuns at Saint Cecilia's convent. When she called to say that she was extending her trip for a few extra days, I felt relieved that she was enjoying herself. As a caregiver for my father, Mom had not traveled for many years, but when she called a few days later to say that she was going to stay a few more days, I became concerned. "What's going on, Mom?" I asked. "Is Aunt Mary alright?" She had been staying with her sister in Davie, near Ft. Lauderdale, "Well, actually, Nance, there's something I want to tell you," Mom replied. "I've met someone. I'm seeing Aunt Mary's brother-in-law, Frank." I responded tentatively, "What does that mean? You're coming home soon, right?" She promised that she would return soon and give me the details when we were together.

When I picked Mom up at the airport, she was glowing and anxious to tell me all about her new companion. She had not been on a date since 1954 and giddily explained that she had been swept off her feet. "He's a retired builder in south Florida who's been alone for a while, and Nance, he's been married several times but said he's never met anyone like me. I can't wait for you to meet Frank. He'll be here on Friday." I was stunned at the pace with which this relationship was developing, but only commented to Mom that I was thrilled to see her happy.

Frank visited my mother twice, flying into Wilkes-Barre/Scranton International Airport for long weekends, before they announced that Mom was selling her house in Harding and moving to Florida. Within a month, Mom left her job at the convent, sold her house, distributed furniture, antiques and presented generous financial gifts to my sister and me. Then, she waved goodbye and drove away to live a life, with Frank, that I thought was beyond her wildest dreams. During the years that Mom sat quietly every night, alone, in her cottage home after Dad's death, I have no doubt that she was visualizing a different, more worldly life.

By securing the substantial Sears account, I believed that at least some of our troubles were behind us at Arpel, however, they were just beginning. We needed money for inventory to stock three hundred and eighty-five new stores and hire additional warehouse employees. One morning, I arrived at our Manhattan office and was quickly pulled into a small office by the head of our sales team, Doug Bowman. "Something big's going on," he said. "I'm not sure, but Mike just had a meeting with Mary and most of the board members. Everyone seems upset." Later that morning, Mary met with Doug and me privately to inform us of the dire financial situation our company was facing. "We don't have the money to open the Sears stores, and I've just been told that we're going to be de-listed by the New York Stock Exchange. The Board is talking about bringing in a turn-around guy."

I had not done my due diligence regarding Arpel's financial stability and had no idea that we were completely out of money. Mary told her staff that, more than ever, we had to be optimistic and put forth a positive image for our customers. She said, "I've got a deal cooking that could change everything if we can get an infusion of cash." A few days later, Gus Wallace, the turn-around guy, took over the conference room and called us in for a huddle. He announced that as his first order of business, he intended to close our Fifth Avenue office and move the entire operation to the New Jersey warehouse. "I've got some money to work with," Wallace said, "Let's see if we can pull ourselves out of this hole."

Mary's deal brought us to QVC headquarters in West Chester, Pennsylvania where we were accompanied by our agent, Ben White, the former president and founder of the Home Shopping Network (HSN). We presented our products and on-air strategy to QVC's CEO, Doug Briggs, and the cosmetics buying team. They loved it and invited us back in two weeks, with our sales plan and financial projections, to potentially close the deal. Ben White whisked me off to Clearwater, Florida, headquarters of the Home Shopping Network, for acting lessons with their top on-air coach. Mary and the finance guys came up with an aggressive sales plan while Doug and I chose skincare products and color palettes that would appeal to QVC's audience. As we traveled to the next meeting at QVC headquarters, Mary and Ben presented me with a contract that outlined the details of my employment as Arpel's television host. I would receive a commission equivalent to half a percent of the first year's projected sales of $30,000,000 and a $25,000 annual clothing budget. I told them, "I'm ready! Let's do this!"

We made our presentation and waited for Briggs' reaction. He had apparently been doing his due diligence because he opened by stating that he was excited about our plans and realized that it would be a significant boost in sales for Arpel. Therefore, in addition to their standard commission, he wanted stock options. He stated firmly that there was no room for negotiation; this was a demand. Arpel's board of directors agreed that there was no room for negotiation; they refused to offer stock options.

It was a glorious Saturday morning when Peter and I walked out onto the front porch toward the street when I noticed that my car was missing. I thought that perhaps I had parked in the back of the house when I picked Helena up from her friend's house the night before. We walked around to the back and there was no car. I went into the house and called the West Pittston Police Department. "Officer, my car has been stolen!" I said frantically. "What's the name and address?" he replied and then followed with "Ma'am, your car's not stolen. It's on the repo list." I went into a panic. "Repo list? What are you talking about?" I asked. "It's a company car and all of my shoes are in the trunk!" The officer replied, "Well, obviously your company didn't pay their bills. Nothing I can do. Sorry. I'll see if I can get your shoes back since you're probably gonna be walking a lot!"

I called Mary, who was spending her weekend in Washington and asked if she knew whether or not the company was in arrears on our car leases. She apologized profusely and authorized me to use my corporate American Express for a rental car. The following Monday morning, Mike Ficke, Arpel's chief financial officer, sent an overnight payment to the leasing company and the next day my car and shoes were returned…but not for long. Mike had only paid one of the missed payments; Arpel had several leased vehicles and the payments were a few months behind. For two weeks, I hid my car in back alleys throughout West Pittston, rather than parking it in front of my house, hoping to stall the next repossession event. During the second week, my paycheck bounced, and a few days later, the car was picked up for the last time.

In what seemed like a flash, I was unemployed, with no savings to fall back on, no car, and two children in high school who were depending upon me to keep it all together. I immediately found a job as a lunch waitress. I took a taxi to and from the restaurant and rode my bicycle for groceries and errands. I promised Peter and Helena that everything would be alright. After all, it was prom season!

Chapter Fourteen

"You may encounter many defeats, but you must not be defeated. In fact, it may be necessary to encounter the defeats, so you can know who you are, what you can rise from, how you can still come out of it."

-Dr Maya Angelou

I had been given the priceless gift of perspective. Peter had already survived six years of cancer treatment; just two more years and he would be declared "cured!"

As part of my study of female survivors of the Holocaust, I was reading *In Memory's Kitchen: A Legacy from the Women of Terezin* which describes how starving women preserved recipes. I had been introduced to Dr. Maya Angelou in *I Know Why the Caged Bird Sings*, wherein Angelou writes about being raped by her mother's boyfriend when she was just a little eight year old girl. In light of my life experience and academic course of study, I felt that, at this point, there was everything to fear regarding my dire financial and employment situation, and nothing to fear when compared to the horrors encountered by the women whose lives I was studying.

I had a life-long track record of disguising stress and anxiety by putting forth a positive image. On the outside, it never appeared as though I was falling apart, but looks could be deceiving. My father, whose father was an alcoholic, forbade alcohol in our home. Mother kept a bottle of Manischewitz wine and peach schnapps in the buffet cabinet for company. I stole my first taste at age ten when my parents allowed my sister and me to stay alone for the first time while they visited relatives in town. The night of my junior prom there was a party in Emma's Trailer Court not far from home. There are photographs of me sitting in a folding chair, head dangling forward, eyes closed, arms limp, in a Boone's Farm wine-stained burgundy gown.

As an adult, about once a year, and on no special occasion, I drank an entire bottle of wine, threw up for two days and didn't touch more than a sip for the rest of the year. It wasn't a coping mechanism, quite the opposite; I was usually dead set on enjoying a few drinks as part of the evening's festivities, but once I got started, something in my mind took over and compelled me to guzzle so much wine that I could not stand up. Fortunately, the shame that followed was so overwhelming that it prevented more frequent occurrences. Thank goodness, I never drank in the middle of a crisis. In retrospect, I seem to have fallen apart after the nightmares were over.

I had begun dating Jay Shaw a few months before I lost my job at Arpel. I believed he was financially secure and he seemed impressed that I was an independent career woman. Jay had been married for thirty-two years before divorcing his wife two years before we met. After losing my job at Arpel and being forced to take a job as a lunch waitress just to keep a roof over my children's heads, I did not ask Jay for financial help, nor did he offer assistance. In fact, although we had been seeing each other exclusively, our dates became less frequent, since I no longer had a car.

Every morning, before leaving for work at the restaurant, I sent out at least twenty cover letters and resumes to cosmetics industry leaders. I ordered an industry directory for $85.00 that listed the names and corporate addresses of each individual company executive. I sent a cover letter and resume to the company president and the vice president of sales. By the end of my first month of unemployment, I had sent almost three hundred resumes and had begun receiving replies. I qualified potential interviews by asking the human resources representative where the open position was located and if it would be possible to conduct business from my home office in northeastern Pennsylvania. By the end of my second month of unemployment, I had completed my second round of interviews with Orlane and Versace and received offers of employment from both companies. In the fall of 1999, I was hired as Versace's metro New York regional sales director.

Giovanni Maria "Gianni" Versace was an Italian fashion designer and founder of Versace, an international fashion house that produces accessories, fragrances, makeup, home furnishings, and clothes. He also designed costumes for theatre and films. He had appointed his brother

Santo, as president, and his sister, Donatella, as vice president of the company in 1978. Gianni Versace was murdered by a serial killer in 1997, shot as he walked outside his mansion in Miami Beach.

At the time Gianni Versace was murdered, he had been preparing to launch his latest venture, a luxurious makeup line exclusive to Bergdorf Goodman and Neiman Marcus. I was responsible for the successful roll-out of the product line, as well as the hiring and training of our retail sales representatives. I was also in charge of the existing fragrance business in Bloomingdale's and Macy's, making the total retail sales responsibility more than $7,000,000. Versace Profumi, while part of the overall brand, operated as a separate entity from couture. I had received a generous compensation package that included salary, expenses, company car, a Versace couture wardrobe twice a year, and a beautiful office on Madison Avenue.

I had only been working for Versace a few weeks when we rendezvoused with the Milan contingent for a sales meeting in Las Vegas. Right after being introduced to the head of public relations and marketing, Antoinette Amici, I met her, again, in the ladies room. Antoinette was a tall, slender, strikingly beautiful blonde woman. She wore a tight black mini skirt with a pair of tan suede boots that covered her knees. It was July in Vegas.

I greeted Antoinette in Italian, my grandmother's Italian, as I stood at the sink in the hotel's nicely appointed powder room. I thought perhaps the chance meeting would give me an opportunity to bond with the Milanese.

Between 1815 and 1871, Italy underwent the challenging process of unification of its diverse provinces. The inhabitants of each region, regardless of social class, conversed in mutually unintelligible dialects. My grandmother, born in 1895, grew up speaking the Foggia version. Foggia, located in an especially beautiful section of Southern Italy, has two towns where an extremely rare dialect of the Franco-Provencal language has been spoken since the 14th century. Today, the dialect is only spoken by 1,400 people in the world.

From my grandmother, I had learned to refer to the bathroom as a *bacavitz* and commented to Antoinette that the hotel *bacavitz* was quite lovely. *"Queste bacavitz es belle."* Ms. Amici looked down at me, disapprovingly, and said sternly, "Ms. VanDermark, you speak beautiful English. Please don't speak to me in Italian again!" My face reddened as I finished washing my hands and quickly exited the ladies room.

Two years later, when my cousin visited from Serracapriola, in the province of Foggia, I explained to him on the drive home from JFK Airport, that I was excited to show him the private room (stanza) and bathroom, *bacavitz,* that would be his for the next month. He shouted, in Italian, "Wait, Nancy! You have a what? A *bacavitz*? You mean the lavatory, the toilet, is outside?"

Alberto explained that the word "*bacavitz*" means "outhouse" and no longer exists in the common vernacular spoken throughout Italy. Grandma's dialect was ancient and did not reflect a "working class" status but, in fact, the lowest "peasant class" status. When I realized why Ms. Amici had chided me on my Italian, in a Vegas bathroom, my face reddened again.

On occasional Friday afternoons, Jay Shaw took a limousine from his home in Connecticut to my office in New York, and accompanied me back to West Pittston for the weekend. It was on one of these wonderful autumn weekends, that Peter came home from high school and proudly announced that he had been elected president of the senior class. I celebrated by tasting a vodka martini for the first time.

Chapter Fifteen

"Change is the end result of all true learning."
-Dr. Leo Buscaglia

"The whole point of being alive is to evolve into the complete person you were intended to be."
-Oprah Winfrey

Throughout my life glamour had been my modus operandi. I had used makeup to achieve temporary, outward change to craft the image I wanted to project to the world. What I wanted more than anything was the permanent transformation that could only be achieved by expanding my mind. If the playing field had been level in 1973 and I had attended college after high school, who might I have become? I believed it was not too late. I realized that if I was willing to risk the security of a full-time, steady job, and give up my health insurance, I could get serious about becoming an educated woman. I sought authenticity through an intellectual pursuit.

In 2000, I applied to Fairfield University, and with my credits from Vermont College accepted, I resigned from my position at Versace and began taking part-time classes as a journalism major. My academic endeavors were supported by a part-time job as a legal assistant for Attorney Alan Senie in Westport, Connecticut. I was thrilled to attend this great Jesuit university by going to regular classes on campus. The professors were outstanding and empathetic, commending my courage to sit in classes during the day alongside traditional age students. Quite often, the students mistook me for a professor, and I found myself frequently explaining my life before college. The students would often respond with, "You've already had the jobs that we're hoping to get!"

I became especially interested in art history and studied it with more enthusiasm than any other subject. The religious and historical context behind great art was completely new to me and, under the direction of Dr. Philip Eliasoph, I received my first "A" and "A+" grades, which I sent to my mother for her refrigerator. I had the incredible experience of traveling to Italy to study art history with Dr. Eliasoph and his wife, Yael, a professor of Italian at the university. The trip was a gift from Jay Shaw who, by then, had become my partner. When I stood inside the Roman Colosseum and at the famous Duomo in Florence, I remembered the small village of Harding where I grew up and its relatively brief American "history." Only a few hundred years before I lived there, it was inhabited by Native Americans; their arrowheads were still found on the riverbank in 1955.

I studied journalism with Jack Cavanaugh, a Pulitzer nominated author and sports writer for *The New York Times*. He helped me to understand that all of my experiences, before arriving on the campus of Fairfield University, were "material" and he encouraged me to write as a reporter. Under his tutelage, I had a feature story published on the front page of *The Connecticut Post* with the byline, "Nancy VanDermark, Correspondent."

Dr. Judy Primavera, my psychology professor, taught me about Abraham Maslow's pyramid of human needs; Maslow was Dyer's mentor. I made the Dean's List for two consecutive years, and decided that finally, the time had arrived to pursue my biggest dream. It was the greatest long-shot ever, and I knew the time was right.

Chapter Sixteen

"I looked up the road I was going and back the way I come, and since I wasn't satisfied, I decided to step off the road and cut me a new path."

-Mrs. Annie Henderson
(Dr. Maya Angelou's grandmother)

On Sunday, August 28, 2005, three months before my fiftieth birthday, I found myself in a strange new place, startled awake by the sound of church bells. I was down the hall from a second-floor bathroom shared by twenty women. As I lay in bed, listening to the unfamiliar sound of dorm life, I became acutely aware of the swing of a heavy wooden door which led to the communal bathroom. Each time the door was shoved open I could hear the muffled sound of steady, hard showers, punctuated by the distinctive roar of loudly flushing commercial toilets. Women's flip-flops briskly slapped the soles of their feet as students walked up and down the hallway outside my door. The only window in my closet-sized eight-by-ten foot room faced west and it gave little clue as to the hour, sending only enough sunlight from behind the white plastic shade to indicate that it was well past dawn.

I sat up and looked around. Before stepping onto the varnished wood floor, I took a few minutes to contemplate my surroundings. The room was strictly utilitarian, furnished with a wooden desk, bookcase, and three-drawer dresser, set against bare, stark white walls. The furniture was old and scratched; I wondered who had been here before me.

My heart began to race as I anxiously considered that, perhaps this time, I had gone too far. I am no stranger to hard work, I thought, but how will I fit in here? I wondered if maybe this was a mistake. I looked at the black and white photographs that Peter and Helena had given to me the last time we were together. "You can do this, Mom," they said lovingly. "It's your turn to become whoever you want to be!" I returned my attention to the room, took a deep breath, and realized that my new life was about to begin.

The room flooded with light as I lifted the window shade. I looked down at the ivy plant that was presented to me upon arrival, then shifted my gaze outside to the stately brick buildings. I smiled, thinking that the scene from my window would have looked the same had I arrived here in the fall of 1973. Chestnut trees stood tall and sturdy, and as their late summer leaves glistened in the sunlight, a warm breeze blew across my face.

I had arrived on the campus of Smith College in Northampton, Massachusetts with nothing more than my clothes and a few cherished mementos. I had been accepted into the Ada Comstock Scholars Program for non-traditional age women, on a full scholarship. I did not have a savings or retirement account, but for the first time in my life, I felt secure. It had taken nearly half a century to rise above fear, insecurity and economic hardship. I finally stood on the only solid ground I had ever felt beneath my feet.

It was announced at dinner that residents of Northrup House should prepare for a meeting at seven o'clock that evening. It was a meet and greet for new students who were asked to share their ideas for the dorm. I volunteered to speak first, and after introducing myself, said, "I'm going to do my room in shabby chic. I think it's perfect for a small space." The girls, all between the ages of eighteen and twenty-one, looked confused before they started laughing. One of the women said, "It's nice to meet you, Nancy. I guess you're an Ada and we love Adas, right everyone? We actually want to talk about ideas for making the transition from home to campus life smooth for our residents, but your decorating sounds great!" That was only the beginning of many red-faced moments!

The fall semester was scheduled to begin in a week. Although given the option of living in a campus apartment, I had chosen to move into a dorm in order to give myself the full experience of attending college. At Smith, students are assigned to a dorm and each house has its own unique cuisine. Residents are given three wonderful meals a day at Julia Child's alma mater, and one may choose to dine at any of the campus dorms. At Northrup House, our chef served strictly vegan vegetarian meals that most of the women found quite satisfying. I, on the other hand, was completely unfamiliar with vegetarianism, having raised my family on meatballs and chicken cutlets, but I decided to keep an open mind about tofu. Mind over matter, I quickly learned, does not apply to gastronomy. My second red-faced moment came when running upstairs, after consuming a soy and tofu concoction that quickly transformed into gas. I was beginning to feel old!

I spent day and night carefully choosing my classes based upon areas of interest and limited prior knowledge. The Dean of our program, Dr. Erika Laquer, recommended that I major in American Studies rather than my selection of Women's Studies, stating that I should consider my degree in terms of broad marketability. This allowed me to take courses in Women's Studies while also pursuing other subjects. She also suggested that I take no more than three, fifteen credit, courses the first semester.

With the thought of law school in my future, I signed up for Constitutional Law but panicked after the first class. The professor was quite impressive, a legal scholar and also very kind. When I apologized and informed her that I was dropping the class because it sounded like Mandarin Chinese, she said, "Please don't, Nancy. I promise that if you stick with it, one day it will click. You've gotten yourself to Smith. I have no doubt that you can handle this class." I dropped it anyway.

I registered for Philosophy 101 with Dr. Jay Garfield, and after reviewing the syllabus, was certain that I had made the right decision. We were going to study Tolstoy's *The Death of Ivan Illych*, a book that Dr. Wayne Dyer had mentioned in so many of his lectures. I was sure that I was in the right place. After the first class, I approached Dr. Garfield and said, "I am honored to be in your class, Dr. Garfield. I am personal friends with the Father of Modern Day Philosophy, Dr. Wayne Dyer." Dr. Garfield looked at me and said, "Who?"

Chapter Seventeen

"Change is the end result of all true learning."
-Dr. Leo Buscaglia

"I've learned that I still have a lot to learn."
-Dr. Maya Angelou

Dr. Robert Weir stood in front of our U.S. history class supported by a PowerPoint presentation that projected an image of an African American man onto the large screen. He asked us to remember Warner Thornton McGuinn whose name had heretofore remained obscure in even the most concise studies of American history.

Samuel Langorne Clemens, writing under the pen name Mark Twain, has occasionally come under attack for his literary characterizations of African Americans. In reality, Clemens was a humanitarian who possessed a distinct consciousness regarding racism in America. He knew that education would significantly level the playing field. Toward that end, Clemens quietly paid for the Yale Law School education of impoverished student Warner Thornton McGuinn, who graduated number one in the class of 1887. McGuinn was only one of many African Americans Clemens sponsored and assisted, both financially and otherwise.

Attorney McGuinn, in turn, became the mentor of a black law school student by the name of Thurgood Marshall. The grandson of a slave, Marshall successfully argued the landmark case, *Brown v. Board of Education*, before the Supreme Court in 1954, which declared school segregation illegal.

During a later class, Dr. Weir introduced his students to a photographic history of lynching in America with a visual presentation based upon the book *Without Sanctuary: Lynching Photography in America*. The book includes an essay by Hilton Als, titled *GWTW* (Gone With the Wind), wherein he describes the danger of being a black man in America. He writes:

In my life as a city dweller, I have crossed dark nighttime streets so as not to make the white woman walking in front of me feel fear. I have deliberately not come up behind a neighbor opening the door to our apartment building, so as not to make him feel what colored people make him feel: robbed, violated, somehow. I have been arrested on my way to school, accused of truancy. Once, when I was coming out of a restaurant with a friend, four or five cops pinned me to a wall, pointing guns at my head. I looked just like someone else.[11]

African Americans were lynched regularly throughout the south, on false charges, in order to maintain white supremacy. Many of the lynchings were considered, by whites, as events to celebrate their status. The lynchings were often held on Sunday afternoons and observers, including children, brought picnic baskets to celebrate the murder of innocents.

When I learned that Hilton Als had been selected as the Smith College 2008 Writer in Residence, I applied for acceptance to his class. Having become known on campus as "the older woman with the pearls," I embraced new opportunities with tremendous trepidation. It had not become easy to subject myself to challenging situations, and although I often felt as though I were steps away from falling off a cliff, I persisted. Als selected me, as one of only ten students, to study with him during my final semester. The other nine students were all of traditional age but they respected my writing voice and Als encouraged my authenticity.

Hilton Als won the 2017 Pulitzer Prize for Criticism and is the theatre critic for *The New Yorker*.

Chapter Eighteen

"Love is the essential existential fact.
It is our ultimate reality and our purpose
on earth. To be consciously aware of it,
to experience love in ourselves and others,
is the meaning of life."
-Marianne Williamson

"If you find it in your heart to care for
somebody else, you will have succeeded."
-Dr. Maya Angelou

In the winter of 2006, I made the decision that my summer would be spent on the Smith College campus where I had been given a wonderful apartment. I applied for a PRAXIS internship as a researcher for a Northampton non-profit, The Breast Form Fund, founded by prominent business owner, Judith Fine.

Ms. Fine, who grew up in Richmond, Virginia, relocated to Massachusetts and opened an exclusive lingerie shop, Gazebo, in the 1970's. A free-spirited, highly artistic intellectual, Ms. Fine is a gorgeous woman with long, white braided hair and a sparkling personality. During the internship interview, she explained that her business had evolved from lingerie, including her original designs, to custom fitted bras and post-mastectomy bras. She said that most insurance plans allocated breast cancer patients with one custom fit bra per year which was hardly adequate. She recognized that women who were uninsured or underinsured were at a complete financial loss for expensive post-mastectomy bras. Therefore, she established a non-profit fund to assist breast cancer survivors in obtaining their bras.

The internship, Ms. Fine explained, would involve visiting every hospital in western Massachusetts to interview the director of social work and conduct additional interviews with nurses in oncologists' offices. If selected, I would also speak directly with patients, and combined with the research findings, determine how much money would be needed to cover the cost of post-mastectomy bras throughout The Pioneer Valley in western Massachusetts, and perhaps the entire state.

Ms. Fine was impressed with my professional background, as a national training director, and with my personal experience as the mother of a child with leukemia. At the conclusion of my interview, she caught me off guard when she abruptly asked me to tell her a joke. I replied quickly, "Condoms aren't completely safe. A friend of mine was wearing one and he got hit by a bus!" She offered me the paid internship and asked me to start as soon as the semester was finished.

In the autumn of my senior year, I received an invitation to high tea at the stately campus home of Carol Christ, President of Smith College, in honor of my status as a First Group Scholar, which ranked me in the top ten percent of the entire student body. I humbly confess that there were not many students at this prestigious event and Dr. Christ took the time to inquire about my personal background and Smith College experience.

"Dr. Christ," I said, "it is the most outstanding privilege of my life to have been included among this group of women and be invited here today. I am the most unlikely scholar in the room!"

I tightened the shawl around my shoulders and walked back to my apartment on Bedford Terrace. I felt good for all of the right reasons. The countless hours of research and writing had produced the desired excellent results. I had become an educated woman. It was real and true and good. No one could ever take it away. I had one more semester to complete before graduation.

I made myself a cup of coffee, a four o'clock in the afternoon ritual that began when I was a young girl waiting for my father to complete his shift. At five o'clock, Helena called, screaming into the phone, "Mom, oh my God, oh my God, oh my God! Dad, it's Dad, he's been in an accident. Mom, it's so bad." She was crying so hard that I had to ask her to breathe. "He's in a helicopter…they're flying him to Scranton Community Medical Center Trauma Unit. He was hit head-on on his motorcycle. Mom, he might not make it."

It was a beautiful early October afternoon. Frank had been enjoying a ride into town on his Harley Davidson, on his way to meet his wife for dinner. As he rounded the turn, from Route 92 onto Exeter Avenue in West Pittston, just blocks before his destination, a drunk thirty-eight-year-old woman, who was going to buy more beer, hit him head-on. Although he was wearing a helmet, Frank suffered a severe traumatic brain injury. The news brought me to my knees. I've stayed there.

When I arrived at the trauma center with my sister, Lynne, we were met by Helena who updated us on Frank's condition. The doctors performed a surgical procedure to stop the bleeding on his brain but the damage was extensive. He needed multiple surgeries to repair broken bones and he had lost the sight in his eye. If he survived, the doctors regretfully informed his wife and Helena, he would never be the same man again.

After his surgeries, Frank was transferred to a rehabilitation facility where he spent several weeks with Helena at his bedside, as he was learning to walk again. During one of our phone calls, I mentioned to Helena that, although her Dad had sworn me to secrecy about his intellectual capabilities many years ago, I had recently been doing research regarding traumatic brain injuries. I learned that people with high I.Q.'s seem to have a greater chance at recovering from that type of injury than do those having average intellect. I related to her the story of the meeting his high school administrators had with Frank's parents when he was still a student. Frank had scored higher on the standard I.Q. test than anyone to whom the school had ever administered the test. I urged Helena to remember that and to never give up hope for her father's recovery.

By mid-December, my final exams were over, and having completed all of the required courses, I had the pleasure of selecting classes that I desired for my final semester at Smith. I was also looking forward to spending time during the winter break with Jay and the children. Jay had just returned from business in Italy and seemed unusually tired. He asked me to accompany him to Memorial Sloan Kettering Cancer Center, on December 19th, for a PET scan that had been ordered by his pulmonologist. It revealed a "shadow" on his right lung that r further investigation.

I returned to Smith in mid-January and immediately went to work my American Studies thesis under the direction of Dr. Daniel Horowitz. Together, we had decided that his work on excessive material consumption, and my background in the cosmetics industry, would produce a unique paper as the capstone of my combined academic and work experience. I returned to Fairfield in mid-February to accompany Jay to Memorial Sloan Kettering for a biopsy. The result was non-small cell lung cancer; surgery was scheduled for April 21st.

In March, I flew to Florida after receiving information that Mom's partner, Roy, had been diagnosed with a rare form of skin cancer and was scheduled for surgery. After Mom's companion, Frank, died, she reconnected with Roy, an acquaintance from Harding whose wife had passed away. Roy was eighty-five years old and did not have any children. He had been diagnosed with Merkle cell carcinoma, a rare form of skin cancer, on his forehead. A surgeon convinced Roy to sign a consent form giving the doctor permission to operate and possibly permanently disfigure Roy's face when they cut open his head from ear to ear. Roy was frightened and asked for my help. I arranged for him to receive treatment at the renowned Cleveland Clinic, in Weston, Florida, where plastic surgeons performed delicate surgery to remove the skin cancer. Sadly, further tests revealed that Roy's cancer had spread to his bones and he died shortly thereafter.

On April 21st I drove Jay to Memorial Sloan Kettering Cancer Center for a laparoscopic procedure to remove the tumor from his lung. Dr. Raja Flores, a world-renowned thoracic surgeon, advised us to prepare for three days at the hospital in Manhattan. Complications from emphysema arose during the operation, thereby eliminating the possibility of a laparoscopic procedure. Instead, Jay required six hours of surgery and a twelve day hospitalization. I stayed in a chair next to Jay's bed and consulted with Dr. Flores daily regarding his condition. On the twelfth day, Dr. Flores stated that the only way he would allow Jay to be discharged was if the nurses trained me to change the

…es on his drainage tube incisions and manage Jay's in-home care …siting nurses. I paid careful attention to the instructions and Jay … discharged on May 3rd.

During the second week of May, Mom went into the Coral Springs Medical Center for a 45-minute stent procedure on a blocked artery in her left leg. It was a week before my long-awaited graduation, but I offered to fly to Florida and accompany Mom to the hospital. "Nance, are you kidding?" she said with her usual optimism. "It's going to be quick, one overnight, so please don't worry about me."

A blood clot formed during the procedure and when I spoke with her by phone, she was crying out in severe pain. Mom was taken back into surgery for a bypass procedure through her groin and then placed in the Intensive Care Unit. She was discharged a few days later unaware that she had contracted MRSA, the deadly staph infection, at the site of her wound. The killer bacteria was eating away at her flesh.

Once again, real life was interrupting academic pursuits. I wondered why I had not studied anatomy instead of astronomy.

Chapter Nineteen

"My mission in life is not to merely survive,
but to thrive; and to do so with some passion,
some compassion, some humor and some style."
-Dr. Maya Angelou

"When a woman rises up in glory, her energy
is magnetic and her sense of possibility contagious."
-Marianne Williamson

On Sunday morning, May 18th, I donned my graduation gown and carefully pinned the cap to my hair. I walked up Bedford Terrace and took my place in line with the Ada Comstock Scholars Class of 2008. As we walked along the commencement route, I saw the radiant, beautiful faces of the people I love so dearly and who supported me throughout the journey. Peter, Helena, and Danny, Helena's boyfriend, ran over to hug and kiss me, followed by my sister, Lynne, brother-in-law-Steve, and three nieces, Sarah, Bethany and Charity. It was a "pinch me I'm dreaming" morning in every way!

My mother and Jay were unable to attend. Mom had offered to pay for a wonderful celebration dinner at Mulino's Trattoria for the entire family and a few close friends. I called her from the restaurant and said, "Mom, I did it! I graduated from Smith College. Can you believe it?" Her voice was shaky as she replied, "Congratulations Nance! I'm so happy for you. You did it – just like Gloria Steinem!"

Epilogue

"Either the United States
will destroy ignorance,
or ignorance will
destroy the United States."
-W.E.B. DuBois

"There is a cult of ignorance in the United States, and there always has been. The strain of anti-intellectualism has been a constant thread winding its way through our political and cultural life, nurtured by the false notion that democracy means that 'my ignorance is just as good as your knowledge.'"

-Isaac Asimov

Throughout my life, I have been inspired by strong women who have experienced poverty and hardship, yet made the difficult decision to pull themselves up and out, toward better opportunities – no matter what it took.

Helen Gurley Brown said that "Good girls go to heaven, bad girls go everywhere," and she also told me to, "Go to college to get an education, to learn how to think, to grow up, but you have to work in a job to learn anything and move to a better one."

Dr. Maya Angelou wrote that:

> *Information helps you to see that you're not alone. That there's somebody in Mississippi and somebody in Tokyo who all have wept, who've all longed and lost, who've all been happy. So the library helps you to see, not only that you are not alone, but that you're not really any different from everyone else.*

Gloria Steinem shared her well-earned wisdom when she said, "What happens at 50, more or less, you lose what you need to create another person, to sustain another person, you keep what you need to sustain yourself. And there's something wonderful about that." At the National Press Club, in 2013, she stated firmly:

> *Don't listen to me.*
> *Listen to yourself...*
> *people often ask me at this age*
> *'Who am I passing the torch to?'*
> *First of all, I'm not giving up my torch, thank you!*
> *I'm using my torch to light other people's torches...*
> *if we each have a torch, there's a lot more light.*

These women realized through their intellect, intuition and foresight that education, personally and for all people is, in fact, the great equalizer.

Prior to studying African American women's history, I had never read primary source accounts of women of color. In *I Know Why the Caged Bird Sings*, Dr. Maya Angelou introduced me to the suffering of African Americans in the Jim Crow South. Regarding her experience with Dr. Lincoln, a white dentist, in Stamps, Arkansas, Angelou recounts that the dentist had borrowed money from Mrs. Annie Henderson, Dr. Angelou's grandmother, affectionately called *Momma*. When Mrs. Henderson approached the dentist about treating her young granddaughter's toothache, he reiterated his policy regarding African Americans. Dr. Angelou writes:

"He was choosing words the way people hunt for shells. 'Annie, you know I don't treat nigra, colored people."

'I know, Dentist Lincoln. But this here is just my little grandbaby and she ain't gone be no trouble to you...'

'Annie, everybody has a policy. In this world you have to have a policy. Now, my policy is I don't treat colored people.'

As the dialogue continues, the dentist states firmly that he had repaid all of the money and that the matter is ended. Mrs. Henderson stands her ground, stating:

'I wouldn't press on you like this for myself but I can't take no. Not for my grandbaby. When you come to borrow my money you didn't have to beg. You asked me, and I lent it. Now, it wasn't my policy. I ain't no moneylender, but you stood to lose this building and I tried to help you out.'

'It's been paid, and raising your voice won't make me change my mind. My policy...' He let go of the door and stepped nearer Momma. The three of us were crowded on the small landing. 'Annie, my policy is I'd rather stick my hand in a dog's mouth than in a nigger's.'[12]

I had been poor – a northeastern Pennsylvania, coal miner's daughter, working-class kind of poor, but being poor and black was entirely different. I understood how it felt to be marginalized in only a fraction of the way racial prejudice affected the lives of black people. When the Light went on, it flooded my mind and I knew, with every fiber of my being, that I have lived the life of a privileged white girl.

If I superimposed a black girl's face onto mine for every opportunity I've had, from childhood to work, and then did the same for the life experiences of my parents and grandparents, discrimination, prejudice, and marginalization are the absolute result.

The racial makeup in Harding, Pennsylvania, when I grew up there in the early 1960's, was 99.8% white; today it is 99.3%. Working class residents of that small village embraced our few African American neighbors as friends. My mother invited migrant workers into our home every summer and at Christmas she received a call from the migrant camp's matriarch, Jesse, in Mississippi.

Since the 1950's, the coal mines shut down, factories closed, and the Mighty Susquehanna has caused historic, catastrophic flooding, several times, causing property values to plummet. The results of capitalism and climate change, at their worst, have transformed a once idyllic "Valley with the Heart," into a region where a new constituency of frustrated, angry residents blame an influx of minorities for everything from an increase in crime to the opioid crisis.

The zeitgeist of ignorance that permeates current American culture, considers higher education elitist and promotes coal mine jobs over re-training. It is dangerous to the working class and poor. Consequently, we are compelled to ask ourselves who benefits from the perpetuation of ignorance and why would anyone want to keep systems in place that push selected groups of people down based upon their skin tone or lack of education and training.

My classmates in the Ada Comstock Scholars Program, women from amazingly diverse backgrounds, sought to become educated. We arrived on the Smith College campus from community colleges, restaurants, offices, and the circus. We worked as hairdressers, school bus drivers, secretaries, homemakers and on the factory assembly line. The stories of our journeys, from the remote farmlands of China and the mountains of Afghanistan, to Smith's Ivy League campus, would astound you. One of my classmates arrived from San Antonio with her husband and three children; Smith College gave the entire family an apartment for three years. Laurie Ann Guerrero has become an award-winning Chicana poet. She was the Poet Laureate of San Antonio from 2014 to 2016 and the Poet Laureate of Texas from 2016 to 2017.

All of my Ada Comstock classmates had their educations interrupted by real life – whether through marriage, divorce, caregiving, or as drop-outs, but each of us demonstrated the ability to keep up with the rigorous Smith College curriculum. We have all been radically transformed by our education. Our personal histories are rich and substantive and we're here to tell the world that we have survived, shattered, battered and, in the words of Dr. Maya Angelou, "and still we rise."

In the years since graduating from Smith, I have become a full-time caregiver and perennial student. My responsibilities have not changed – I clean the house, cook the meals, do the laundry, manage the medical care, and sometimes feel socially isolated and lonely. I take classes in Constitutional Law, Holocaust Studies, political science and writing at the University of Delaware Lifelong Learning Center. I continue to use my critical thinking skills to examine the world through the lens of white privilege. The term "white privilege" was never articulated, by any of my professors, at any institution of higher learning. My "privilege," by virtue of skin tone, in a system constructed to designate "white" as superior to other shades, became apparent through a synthesis of information that I was required to carefully analyze. It includes history, sociology, anthropology, religion, and science.

The path has been rocky and I have stumbled…often. The poet Leonard Cohen writes:

> *Ring the bells that still can ring.*
> *Forget your perfect offering.*
> *There is a crack in everything.*
> *That's how the light gets in.*

I am deeply grateful to Smith College and all of the wonderful people who have illuminated my path with knowledge and understanding. I have been humbled by the messes I've made as I journey through life. The cracks formed, whether by choice or chance, and I have chosen to be guided by the Light.

I leave you with the following wisdom from C.S. Lewis:

> *You can't go back and change the beginning*
> *but you can start*
> *where you are and change*
> *the ending.*

Bibliography

1. *Wikipedia.* Retrieved July 1, 2018 from http://wikipedia.org/HouseofLaMarck.

2. Anne of Cleves. *HistoryExtra.* Retrieved July 1, 2018 from http://historyextra.com/period/tudor/anne-of-cleves-henry-viiis-most-successful-queen.

3. DuBois, Ellen Carol and Dumenil, Lynn, *Through Women's Eyes: An American History with Documents*, Boston: Bedford/St. Martin's, 2009, p. 535.

4. Italian Immigration. Retrieved July 1, 2018 from http://www.pbs.org/destinationamerica/usim_wn_noflash_5.html.

5. DuBois, Ellen Carol and Dumenil, Lynn, *Through Women's Eyes: An American History with Documents*, Boston: Bedford/St. Martin's, 2009, p. 410.

6. "Local History: Harding Massacre of 1778," The Times Tribune (June 29, 2014) by Erin Nissley.

7. DuBois, Ellen Carol and Dumenil, Lynn, *Through Women's Eyes: An American History with Documents*, Boston: Bedford/St. Martin's, 2009, pp. 595, 596.

8. DuBois, Ellen Carol and Dumenil, Lynn, *Through Women's Eyes: An American History with Documents*, Boston: Bedford/St. Martin's, 2009, p. 670.

9. Steinem, Gloria, *Revolution from Within: A Book of Self Esteem*, Boston: Little, Brown and Company, 1992, p. 110.

10. Dyer, Wayne W., *You'll See It When You Believe It: The Way to Your Personal Transformation*, New York: William Morrow, 1989, pp. 14, 15.

11. Allen, James; Als, Hilton; Lewis, Congressman John; Litwack, Leon F., *Without Sanctuary: Lynching Photography in America*, Santa Fe: Twin Palms Publishers, 2008, pp. 40, 41. (GWTW is copyright Hilton Als, 2000).

12. Angelou, Maya, *I Know Why the Caged Bird Sings*, New York: Random House Trade Paperback Edition, 1969, 1997 by Maya Angelou Reading Group Guide, copyright 2009 by Random House, Inc.

Sources of Knowledge and Inspiration

Dr. Jill Ker Conway was the first woman president of Smith College. She served from 1975 to 1985 during which time she developed the groundbreaking "Ada Comstock Scholars Program," an innovative, life-changing and highly regarded program for students beyond the traditional age. Dr. Conway authored three memoirs:
The Road from Coorain, True North and *A Woman's Education.*
All "were critically praised, and all were best sellers, focusing, as Conway said, on 'what women were not supposed to acknowledge – ambition, love of adventure, the quest for intellectual power, physical courage and endurance, risk taking, the negative aspects of mother/daughter relations always so relentlessly sentimentalized.'" *Smith College website*

Ada Comstock graduated from Smith College in 1897. In 1923, she was inaugurated as president of Radcliffe College, where "she spent 20 years leading the school, strengthening its academic programs and, in 1943, persuaded Harvard to accept classroom co-education." "The largest collection of her papers, 1897-1950, are housed at the Smith College Archives." *Wikipedia*

Sophia Smith founded Smith College in 1870 with the substantial estate she inherited from her father, a wealthy farmer. Smith decided, after much deliberation and advice, that leaving her inheritance to found a women's college was the best way for her to fulfill the moral obligation she expressed so eloquently in her will: 'I hereby make the following provisions for the establishment and maintenance of an Institution for the higher education of young women, with the design to furnish for my own sex means and facilities for education equal to those which are afforded now in our colleges to young men." *Wikipedia/Smith College website*

Dr. Erika Laquer was the Dean of the Ada Comstock Scholars Program at Smith College throughout my education at Smith. She holds a Ph.D. in history from the University of Pennsylvania and is also a doula who helps women before, during and after they give birth. "In both roles, she says, she is at the sides of women as they create new lives." (*Daily Hampshire Gazette*, Sunday, October 28, 2012).

Paula J. Giddings, professor of Afro-American studies, introduced me to Ida B. Wells- Barnett. Her book, *Ida: A Sword Among Lions*, won the *LA Times* Book Prize for Biography. Professor Giddings' work chronicles the lifelong anti-lynching activism of Wells-Barnett. Imagine the shock when students learned that in 2007 there was still no anti-lynching legislation passed in the United States. She is also the author of:
When and Where I Enter: The Impact on Black Women on Race and Sex in America;
In Search of Sisterhood: Delta Sigma Theta and the Challenge of the Black Sorority Movement.
Smith College Website

Dr. Neal Salisbury (Ph.D., UCLA) is Professor Emeritus of History at Smith College and specializes in Native American and colonial American history, particularly in New England. He began his first day of lecturing on Native American history by asking the class how many indigenous people we thought inhabited the North American continent pre-contact, before the arrival of Christopher Columbus and the white Europeans. Our answers ranged from 10,000 to 100,000 with a few students speculating that perhaps there were only a few hundred. Dr. Salisbury's research revealed that there were between 7,000,000 and 10,000,000 indigenous people on the continent in 1492 and, that by the 1860 U.S. census (excluding Alaska), there were less than 350,000.

Dr. Salisbury is the author of:
"Spiritual Giants, Worldly Empires: Indigenous Peoples and New England to the 1680's," in *The World of Colonial America: An Atlantic Handbook* (2017),
"The Atlantic Northeast," in *The Oxford Handbook of American Indian History* (2014),

and *Manitou and Providence: Indians, Europeans, and the Making of New England, 1500-1643* (1982). He coauthored *The People: A History of Native America* (2007) – MacMillan Learning.

Dr. Salisbury is considered throughout the world to be one of the foremost experts on Native American history.
Smith College Website

Dr. Ginetta Candelario, author of *Black Behind the Ears: Dominican Racial Identity from Museums to Beauty Shops*, was my professor for sociology and Latin American Feminism. She serves on the advisory group for the Gloria Steinem & Wilma Mankiller School for Organizers at Smith College. She has been a Fulbright Scholar in the Dominican Republic twice, in 2003 and 2016, and is the author of *Miradas desencadenantes: Los estudios de genero en la Republica Dominicana al inicio del tercer milenio,* which was the first published collection of gender and women's studies research in the Dominican Republic and spurred a biennial publication series by the Center for Gender Studies (CEG) at the Instituto Tecnologico in Santo Domingo. Candelarios' work has appeared in numerous interdisciplinary journals.
Smith/Wikipedia websites

Dr. Jennifer Guglielmo is a writer, historian and professor at Smith College specializing in the histories of labor, race, women, immigration, transnational cultures and activism, and revolutionary social movements in the modern United States. She is the author of the award-winning book *Living the Revolution: Italian Women's Resistance and Radicalism in New York City, 1880-1945* and co-editor (with Salvatore Salerno) of *Are Italians White? How Race is Made in America*. The book was translated into Italian in 2006: *Gli Italiani Sono Bianchi? Come l' American ha construito la razza*. Her work has been funded by the Social Science Research Council and the American Association of University Women. She is currently translating short essays written in Italian by immigrant women anarchists in early twentieth-century New York City and northeastern New Jersey, which will be reprinted in her

next book, *My Rebellious Heart: Immigrant Women's Anarchist Feminist Prose in New York City's Radical Subculture, 1890-1930.*
Smith/Wikipedia websites

Dr. Gwendolyn Mink, has been teaching U.S. equality law, poverty policy, gender issues, and American politics for twenty nine years. She was on the faculty of Smith College from 2001 to 2009. She is the author of *Welfare's End*, a Choice magazine 'Outstanding Academic Book;' *Hostile Environment*, *The Wages of Motherhood*, which won the 1996 Victoria Schuck Book Award of the American Political Science Association; and *Old Labor and New Immigrants in American Political Development.* She is editor of *Whose Welfare?*; co-editor (with Wilma Mankiller, Marysa Navarro, Barbara Smith and Gloria Steinem) of *The Reader's Companion to U.S. Women's History*; co-editor (with Rickie Solinger) of *Welfare: A Documentary History of Policy and Politics*; and co-editor (with Alice O'Connor) of *Poverty An Encyclopedia of History, Politics, and Policy.*
Smith College Website

Dr. Helen Lefkowitz Horowitz introduced me to Theodore Drieser's classic American novel, *Sister Carrie*. Dr. Horowitz's research ranges over a number of areas: urban life, cultural philanthropy, women, higher education, biography, sexuality, sexual representation, censorship, intimate life, understandings of health and illness, understanding of the landscape and tourism. Horowitz was editor of *Landscape in Sight: J.B. Jackson's America* and co-editor of *Love Across the Color Line: The Letters of* Alice *Hanley*. She has authored several books including:
A Taste for Provence,
Wild Unrest: Charlotte Perkins Gilman and the Making of the Yellow Wallpaper, and *Rereading Sex: Battles Over Sexual Knowledge and Supression in Nineteenth Century America.*
Smith College Website

Dr. Daniel Horowitz was my senior advisor. He introduced me to Dr. Kathy Peiss, Chair of the History Department at the University of Pennsylvania and author of *Hope in a Jar: The Making of America's*

Beauty Culture. My presentation, "A History of Cosmetics in America," based upon Dr. Peiss's work, was selected for the 2016 Women's Leadership Conference at Smith College.

Dr. Horowitz is an historian whose work focused on the history of consumer culture and social criticism in the United States during the 20th century. He directed the American Studies Program at Smith College, for 18 years where he was a distinguished professor. Dr. Horowitz is the recipient of numerous honors including two fellowships from the National Endowment for the Humanities and one from the National Humanities Center; an appointment as Honorary Visiting Fellow at the Schlesinger Library, Radcliffe College, Harvard University and a fellowship from the John Simon Guggenheim Memorial Foundation.

Dr. Horowitz's publications include:
The Morality of Spending: Attitudes Toward the Consumer Society in America, selected by Choice as one of the outstanding academic books of 1985;
Vance Packard and America Social Criticism;
Betty Friedan and the Making of The Feminine Mystique: The American Left, The Cold War, Modern Feminism;
The Anxieties of Affluence: Critiques of American Consumer Culture, selected by Choice as one of the outstanding books of 2004 and winner of the Eugene M. Kayden Prize for the best book published in the humanities in 2004 by a university press;
Consuming Pleasures: Intellectuals and Popular Culture in the Postwar World; and
On the Cusp: The Yale College Class of 1960 and a World on the Verge of Change.
Smith College Website

Dr. Floyd Cheung was my second year American Studies adviser. He teaches courses in American Literature, American Studies and Asian American Literature and Culture. Cheung has published numerous articles in academic journals and also writes poetry. His edited volumes

include H. T. Tsiang's novel *And China Has Hands*; *Sadakichi Hartmann: Collected Poems, 1886-1944* and H. T. Tsiang's novel *The Hanging on Union Square*. His essays include "Reclaiming Mobility: Japanese American Travel Writing after the Internment;" "Negative Attraction: The politics of Interracial Romance in The Replacement Killers" and "*Les Cenelles* and Quadroon Balls: Hidden Transcripts of Resistance and Domination in New Orleans, 1803-1845."
Smith College Website

Dr. Jay Garfield was my philosophy professor when I studied "The Meaning of Life" during my first year at Smith College. During my senior year, Dr. Garfield brought His Holiness the Dalai Lama to Smith for a private audience with students.

Dr. Garfield directs Smith's Logic and Buddhist Studies programs and the Five College Tibetan Studies in India program. His is also visiting professor of Buddhist Philosophy at Harvard Divinity School, professor of philosophy at Melbourne University and adjunct professor of philosophy at the Central University of Tibetan Studies.

Garfield's most recent books are:
Minds Without Fear: Philosophy in the Indian Renaissance;
Dignaga's Investigation of the Percept: A Philosophical Legacy in India and Tibet;
Engaging Buddhism: Why it Matters to Philosophy, and
Moonpaths: Ethics and Emptiness.
Smith College Website

Dr. Robert Weir (Ph.D., University of Massachusetts Amherst) teaches U.S. History at Smith College and is currently the executive secretary of the Northeast Popular/American Culture Association and an associate editor of the *Historical Journal of Massachusetts*. He was a senior Fulbright scholar in New Zealand. Dr. Weir has published seven books on American social and labor history including:
Beyond Labor's Veil: The Culture of the Knights of Labor
Knights Unhorsed: Internal Conflict in a Gilded Age Social Movement

The Historical Encyclopedia of American Labor (with James Hanlan)
Knights Down Under: The Knights of Labour in New Zealand
Class in America
Smith College Website

Annie Boutelle, has been a member of the English Department at Smith College since 1984. "She heeded Ruth Simmons's 1996 call to 'dream big dreams,' envisioning a program to bring an ongoing stream of distinguished poets to Smith. Faculty, students, and alumnae responded enthusiastically, and thus the Poetry Center was born. Boutelle serves as its chair and as a Senior Lecturer Emerita in English Language and Literature.

She is the author of *Thistle and Rose: A Study of Hugh MacDiarmid's Poetry* and scholarly and popular articles on wide-ranging topics. Her new books are collections of poems: *Becoming Bone* is based on the life of 19th century American poet Celia Thaxter, and *Nest of Thistles*, winner of the Samuel French Morse Poetry Prize, focuses on her Scottish childhood.
Smith College Website

The Sophia Smith Collection at Smith College is an internationally recognized repository of manuscripts, archives, photographs, periodicals and other primary sources in women's history. It was founded in 1942 to be the library's distinctive contribution to the college's mission of educating women.

The Collection consists of over 10,700 linear feet of material in manuscript, print and audiovisual formats. There are over 700 individual collections in all.

Subject strengths include birth control and reproductive rights; women's rights; suffrage; the contemporary women's movement across race, class, and sexual orientation; U.S. women working abroad; the arts, especially theatre; the professions, especially journalism and social work; and middle-class family life in nineteenth- and twentieth-century New England.

The Collection houses the complete works of Helen Gurley Brown and Gloria Steinem as well as the periodicals *Cosmpolitan* and *Glamour*.
Smith College Website

Dr. James Lowenthal teaches astronomy at Smith College. He researches high redshift galaxies, Lyman break galaxies, starburst galaxies, millimeter and submillimeter galaxies, galaxy formation and evolution, QSO absorption line systems, QSO host galaxies and ultra-faint radio sources.

His publications include "X-ray detections of submillimeter galaxies: active galactic nuclei versus starburst contribution," "The VLT LBG Redshift Survey- 11. Interactions between galaxies and the IGM at z-3," "Color-Magnitude Relation and Morphology of Low-Redshift ULIRGs in Sloan Digital Sky Survey," and "AzTEC half square degree survey of the SHADES fields-1. Maps, catalogues and source counts."

Dr. Lowenthal sat with me, patiently, as I cried in frustration, while attempting algebraic calculations to determine distance, time and space between selected stars. He taught me how to detect satellites on the Smith College rooftop observatory. He is an angel.
Smith College Website

Dr. Alfonso Procaccini's class "La Dolce Vita" was an intensive study of Italian culture with an expert. A native of Italy, Dr. Procaccini earned his doctorate in Italian literature at Johns Hopkins University, which included two years of study at the University of Florence, Italy. Following six years of teaching at Yale University, he joined the Smith faculty in 1981. He has directed the Smith Program Abroad in Florence, Italy, numerous times.

Procaccini's work includes studies on Dante, Boccaccio, Alberti, Machiavelli, Galileo, Manzoni, Pirandello, Pavese and Pasolini. He is

currently working on a book concerned with the theme of wonder and the poet's peculiar vision in various Italian authors from Dante to Galileo.
Smith College Website

Dr. Peter N. Gregory received his Ph.D. in East Asian Languages and Civilizations from Harvard University and has focused his research on Buddhism in America. He produced a film, *The Gate of Sweet Nectar: Feeding Hungry Spirits in an American Zen Community,* and co-edited a book, *Women Practicing Buddhism: American Experiences*. While studying "Zen in America" with Dr. Gregory, he brought renowned "Beat" poet Gary Snyder for an up close, intimate Q & A with our class of twenty students.
Smith College Website

Dr. Philip Eliasoph gave me the first "A" on a term paper that I had received as an adult college student. His art history classes at Fairfield University, are nothing short of life-altering both in content and presentation.

In 2016 Dr. Eliasoph was invited to design and author his own blog featuring Art History & Visual Culture for the *InEducation* digital platform of *The New York Times*. He is an elected member of the Association Internationale des Critiques d'Art, *UNESCO's* art critic organization based in Paris

Dr. Eliasoph's numerous books, exhibition catalogs, magazine articles, and countless reviews as an active art critic have sparked the rediscovery of American masters including Paul Cadmus, Robert Vickrey, Stevan Dohanos, Colleen Browning, Robert Bizinsky, Henry Koerner and Adolf Dehn.

Whether teaching Florentine painting, WPA urban romanticism, modern abstractionism, or the peculiar dynamics of the contemporary art market and auction scene, he passionately encourages audiences to appreciate why '*ART REALLY MATTERS*!'

Fairfield University Website

Jack Cavanaugh was my journalism professor at Fairfield University. He was a longtime sportswriter for *The New York Times* after working as a news reporter for ABC News and CBS News. He is the author of the Pulitzer-Prize-nominated *Tunney*, a book about former heavy-weight champion Gene Tunney, and *Giants Among Men*, a book detailing the rise of the New York Giants in the mid and late-1950s and early 1960s.

Under the direction of Professor Cavanaugh, I had a feature story on the Bridgeport-Port Jefferson Ferry published on the front page of *The Connecticut Post*. Professor Cavanaugh encouraged me to expand and publish an essay, written under his tutelage, into a book. *Mountain Hawk: I Won't Give Up, A Story of Hope*, published in May 2018, chronicles my son's cancer journey. I am forever grateful for Professor Cavanaugh's inspiration.
Fairfield University Website

Acknowledgements

I am deeply grateful to my wonderful editor, Cynthia Gurin, for her expertise, support and loving-kindness throughout the writing and editorial process. Without Ms. Gurin, this book would not have been born. (http://www.TheQuantumCat.com).

My heart overflows with love and gratitude for my parents, Helen and Emmit VanDermark, whose steadfast love gave me strength and determination.

Thank you to my sister, Lynne VanDermark Cast, who shares so many of these stories and whose wonderful love keeps our family together.

Thank you, Jay Shaw. Your love and friendship made me stronger.

I would like to express my heartfelt appreciation to all of the extraordinary people who have offered me a hand up and out and especially to the phenomenal women who have demonstrated that intelligence, self-esteem, and loving-kindness can coexist.

I am eternally grateful for the unconditional love from my children, Peter and Helena Castellino.

Milton Keynes UK
Ingram Content Group UK Ltd.
UKHW012350161123
432713UK00003B/28/J

9 781644 381779